PEOPLE OF THE EARTH

MYSTICAL ENCOUNTERS
IN AOTEAROA NEW ZEALAND

Prophecy on the River
Judith Hoch

The Luminous Nun
Kerryn Levy

The Lantern in the Skull
Hugh Major

People of the Earth
Peter Calvert, Richard Bentley
Carolyn Longden, Trisha Wren

RELATED PUBLICATIONS

The Matapaua Conversations
Peter Calvert and Keith Hill

The New Mysticism
Keith Hill

PEOPLE OF THE EARTH

Ecology, survival and nurturing spirits

Peter Calvert, Richard Bentley
Carolyn Longden, Trisha Wren

Transcribed by Peter Calvert and Trisha Wren
Edited by Keith Hill

attar books

First edition published in 2019 by Attar Books
Auckland, New Zealand.

Casebook ISBN 978-0-9951203-6-5
Paperback ISBN 978-0-9951203-7-2
Ebook ISBN 978-0-9951203-8-9

Cover image: Sarayat Sy/Shutterstock

AgapeSchoolinz website
www.agapeschool.nz

Attar Books is a New Zealand company that focuses on writing that explores
today's spiritual and mystical experiences, culture, concepts and practices. For
more information on Attar Books' publications visit the website:

www.attarbooks.com

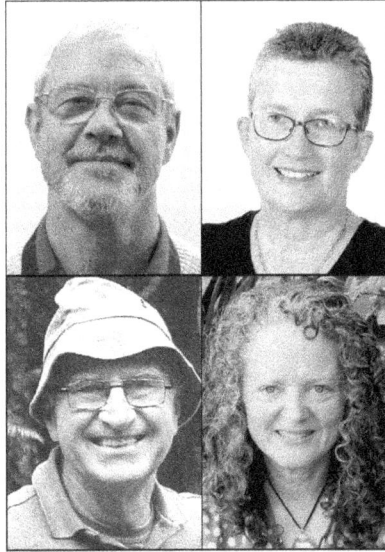

The authors, clockwise from top left:

Peter Calvert worked professionally as an engineering research associate and has extensive experience in Buddhist Vipassana meditation, Spiritualist platform mediumship and holotropic breathwork. After learning to write while in a meditative state, he began communicating with non-embodied identities who sought to transfer their knowledge into written form. The year 1998 proved a watershed. Peter began leading meditation groups, and also started channelling material intended to provide a new perspective on spiritual practices and metaphysical ideas suited to contemporary seekers. This perspective included new terminology, metaphors and models that update ancient spiritual understanding as described in the Hindu, Buddhist and Taoist traditions. Peter has established Agapeschoolinz to share what he is discovering, and is the author of a number of books on spiritual topics. *The Matapaua Conversations* (2013), co-written with Keith Hill, was a finalist in New Zealand's Ashton Wylie Award for spiritual writing. Peter lives in Gore, New Zealand, with his partner, Janet.

Carolyn Longden began her spiritual journey with the discovery of the energy of colour. After becoming aware of the power of energy healing, and shifting to Hamilton, Carolyn was invited to attend a friend's meditation group. Without any prior knowledge of channelling, Carolyn found herself completely "at home". Carolyn continues to live in Hamilton, New Zealand, where she operates a business as a colour consultant and personal stylist.

Trisha Wren is a lifelong animal and horse person. After learning Reiki techniques, she became increasingly interested in listening to what horses were trying to say. Joining an established meditation group opened up spiritual connections she had previously considered out of reach, including her abilities as an animal communicator. She now works as an animal communicator and healer, specialising in horses and their energetic balance. Trisha lives in Cambridge, New Zealand, with her husband Ian and their animal family.

Richard Bentley, a wordsmith with a science background, has an ongoing curiosity about unseen energies and entities. He quizzes such "visitors" with compassion and tongue-in-cheek humour to keep the tone warm and welcoming. Richard writes about agriculture and science from the Waikato, where he lives with his wife Rosie.

Contents

Exploring the Extra-Normal

Philosopher and psychologist, William James, considered our everyday waking consciousness to be just one special state of consciousness among the many states human beings may potentially experience. Of non-everyday states, he was especially interested in religious, spiritual and mystical feelings, and psychic, mediumistic and paranormal perceptions. His stance was that no account of human psychology is complete that leaves these out of consideration.

In his ground-breaking study, *The Varieties of Religious Experience*, James concluded that these experiences, which he termed extranormal (in the sense of being beyond normal waking experience), are typically brief and elusive, occur outside the activity of the rational intellect, and are impossible to put into words. James broke the ground for the psychological exploration of extra-normal states. Since his time, significant research has been carried out, using psychedelics, shamanic trance techniques and meditation to induce extra-normal states at will. Extensive data has also been collected from people who have reported having had near death and out-of-body experiences.

This book adds to the growing body of contemporary research. It presents the records of meditation sessions held by a group based in Hamilton, New Zealand. The sessions occurred over a period of six months, from November 2013 to May 2014. The group was founded in 1998 by Peter Calvert and several colleagues who shared an interest in meditation. Membership of the group changed over the years, but numbers were never large, with the 2013 and 2014 sessions involving between two and six meditators.

All sessions began with participants sitting in a circle, closing their eyes, and entering an inwardly focused state. A guided meditation then aligned everyone's awareness. The sessions' purpose was to open communication with non-corporeal beings. Such beings have long been referred to as spirits. A widespread assumption is that many spirits intend harm. Chinese and Japanese traditions maintain the deceased may become a "hungry ghost" who harasses the living, while contemporary horror films and paranormal television shows overwhelmingly depict spirits as out to "get" whoever enters their haunts.

The Hamilton meditators encountered no such beings. Instead, their most common interaction was with deceased human beings who were unsure what they should do next. The following, transcribed from a meeting held on 7 November 2013, reflects a typical encounter:

> T Someone else is here. I feel a bit queasy. *I'm scared.*
>
> K Why are you scared? Was someone frightening you?
>
> T *As soon as you started talking to me the fear went away.*
>
> K That's good. There's no need to be scared any more. What was making you afraid?
>
> *I was afraid because I was alone. But now you people are here.*
>
> You don't need to be alone any more. You have friends and family waiting for you. Did you know you can move on?
>
> *It sounds familiar.*
>
> You've probably done it before, in past lives. You just need to go to the light. Can you see the light?
>
> *Yes, there's some sort of sunrise.*
>
> Just float towards the sunrise. It will get brighter and brighter. It will soon envelop you. You'll feel so light and free.
>
> *It feels bright and warm after being dark and alone.*
>
> That's good. Just keep going forward. *[Gone.]*

This is a word-for-word transcript of what was said. Each meditator wore a microphone so what was spoken during a session could be recorded for later transcription. In this and the transcripts that follow, the letters—here "T" and "K"—identify individual meditators. The italicised text consists of what the non-corporeal visitor spoke through one of the meditators. The exchanges took the form of questions and answers, with one meditator performing the role of lead questioner. Once the speakers have been established in each transcription, the letter identifiers are dropped to enhance readability.

The above encounter is popularly known as a soul rescue. Each rescue involves helping a lost or confused deceased person move on to the next phase of their afterlife existence. However, the meditators encountered many other types of non-corporeal beings. Some claimed to be from other planets. Several said they had never lived in a body. One of the most significant categories of non-corporeal beings encountered consisted of those who associate with plant and animal species on Earth, or with the planet's physical environments and their ecosystems. These beings are commonly known as nature spirits.

The meditators' encounters with nature spirits suggest that they have long been misunderstood. Traditional accounts of nature spirits, available in religious texts, myths and folk stories told around the world, have invariably described them from a human perspective, in terms of how they affected the human beings they encountered. I have come across no traditional accounts in which nature spirits describe what they do entirely from their own perspective.

What additionally taints traditional accounts of nature spirits is, as noted earlier in relation to ghosts, that they are customarily viewed fearfully. This is illustrated in Aotearoa by stories Māori tell about taniwha. In many locales taniwha are revered as kaitiaki (protective guardians) of rivers, harbours and underground caverns. However, stories from ancient times also described taniwha as predatory monsters who ate people and kidnapped women for sex. As has traditionally been done with "hungry ghosts", placatory offerings were made to taniwha by those who needed to pass through their territory. Alternatively, if a taniwha created too much trouble, brave warriors were assigned to tame or kill it.

Traditional accounts never depict nature spirits in their own terms. What they do in the natural world is not described, and their ecological functions are at best conceived only generally. The following records remedy that lack. Their most significant feature is that the meditators have given the nature spirits who joined them the opportunity to describe what they do and want *from their own perspective.*

This in itself is momentous. However, the meditators didn't stop there. The group also took on the task of identifying varieties of nature spirits, establishing the range of their activities, and defining the scales on which they act. A vision one of the group had during a meeting held on 19 December, 2013, outlines their approach:

> C I'm getting visuals. Lots of white, like snow. Someone is walking through. Footprints in the white. Tentative footsteps. Each step represents us as a group. We're taking steps into this vast, pure, pristine wilderness. It's trackless. No one's been there before. But there's guidance, like a compass.
>
> P Are we to map that territory?
>
> C We will experience that area of knowledge. It's a specific class of study. Our steps are being guided as we explore the territory. Now I see the area has turned green. It's sprouting trees and plants, rivers, mountains. It's still a white canvas, but we're in this green space.
>
> P Have we brought growth?
>
> C No. This is the region we're investigating. We've started walking in the territory of elementals, elementals of the earth, trees, rivers. As a group we're in there. There's wide open spaces ready for us to investigate, search, research. We can lift up things and look underneath. Ask questions. It's ready for us. The answers are there. Our inquisitiveness will lead us to classify it so we can understand. All the entities living there are available to us, so we can learn about the whole living spectrum and assist it in its continued existence.

This vision offers three insights into the groups' explorations of nature spirits. The first is that the group was being aided in their explorations by non-corporeal beings. These beings functioned as guides who engineered encounters between the meditators and individual nature spirits. The second point is that the guides dropped the traditional term of *nature spirit* in favour of *elemental*. Third, the group was invited to draw on their curiosity to explore elementals' domains in depth. The vision suggests they were being provided with an opportunity to explore any territory they wished and question any entity they found dwelling there. The group's following up of this invitation fills a significant portion of the following pages.

From these descriptions, it is clear that the traditional term *spirit* doesn't adequately describe the diversity of beings the meditators encountered. An alternative term, such as *non-embodied identity*, is useful here. Unlike *spirit*, it doesn't have the negative associations we almost automatically project onto such beings. Rather, *non-embodied identity* is an open signifier, creating space for the future differentiation of non-corporeal beings into categories equivalent to biological genus, species and family.

The meditators' reports also counter the assumption that non-embodied identities are inherently a threat to human beings. Some identities the meditators encountered were indifferent to humanity's existence, some were curious about what the group was doing, some sought their help, and some offered insights into the diversity of non-embodied existence. A major contributor to this last category are Peter Calvert's guides—although *guides* is another term that is too generic to adequately reflect the actual variety of non-embodied guides the meditators record having encountered, and the differences in their expertise. For example, one reported guide is an elemental named Mica who introduced the group to other elementals. In comparison, Peter's guides say they are human beings who have completed their cycle of incarnations. Not only did they engineer encounters with other non-embodied identities, they provided models to help group members understand the different natures of non-embodied identities. A number of these models are included in the appendices.

The elephant in the room, of course, is the question of whether the meditators really did communicate with non-embodied beings. Do non-embodied identities exist? If so, do they possess awareness, volition and intelligence? Obviously, what prevents serious consideration of these questions is that they conflict with the materialist approach assumed by the sciences, and the demonisation of spiritual identities in religious and folk traditions, which makes them something to run from rather than engage with. Non-embodied beings are also out of sync with the commodification of nature's output practised by the agricultural industries, and with the down-to-earth "if you can't touch it, it doesn't exist" outlook we New Zealanders pride ourselves in possessing.

This series of books is dedicated to challenging these assumptions. Each writer presents accounts of their extra-normal perceptions. The records offered in *People of the Earth* are presented without comment, so readers may form their own response to what the meditators encountered. If this book presents one central idea, it is that human beings are not the only beings existing on this planet who possess awareness, identity and volition, or who engage creatively with the environment. There are many other beings, who henceforth may collectively be identified as people of the Earth.

As yet, humanity's view of reality is almost exclusively focused on human beings. Indeed, given humanity's exploitative treatment of other species, and our fearful resistance to engaging with the spiritual Other, accepting species diversity as including both corporeal and non-corporeal beings will take considerable time. Meanwhile, intrepid explorers, like this group of meditators, are leading us into territory that remains fascinatingly informative regarding who else is here with us, however strange the resulting encounters.

It is only by acknowledging the "out there", no matter how unclear we are regarding what precisely "out there" encompasses, that we may come to appreciate we are part of an interlinked network of beings who collectively sustain the planet. Physical and non-physical, seen and unseen, acknowledged and unacknowledged ... together, we are all people of the Earth.

— Keith Hill, series editor

PEOPLE OF THE EARTH

The meditators

A list of those who attended the meditation sessions follows, along with their single letter identifiers. Those attending sessions varyied between two and six in number, the average being four. The *italised text* is communication channelled by one of the meditators:

Core group of meditators:

C	Carolyn Longden
P	Peter Calvert
R	Richard Bentley
T	Trisha Wren

Occasionally present:

B	Craig Boyte
K	Karen Hoover

An Evening of Soul Rescues

T *I'm feeling worried and scared, but I'm not supposed to speak. I'm so scared I'm digging my nails into my palms.*

C Has someone else told you not to speak?

T *No. I'm ashamed to speak.*

P All issues of shame can be safely left behind. What could not be spoken of now can be. We do not condemn.

I can never be forgiven for that.

C Why is forgiveness even necessary?

Maybe I can't forgive myself.

P Try it. Provocation can sometimes be overwhelming.

I killed my husband.

Some wives do that. Why did you?

He pushed me too far.

Could you not consider that a form of self-defence?

It wasn't self-defence. I suffocated him in his sleep.

R What provoked you to do that?

Mental abuse.

So it was a form of self-protection?

More than twenty-five years.

P Are you supposed to be all-forgiving without limit?

No, but killing someone isn't okay. I should have left him. I wasn't strong enough to leave.

When did this happen?

1800s, in Wales.

R Your shame must have been intense. It's now the twenty-first century. Are you ready to move on now?

Maybe this is what I deserve.

You deserve to move on.

Maybe I'll just be stuck here forever.

There's no reason for you to remain here any longer. Look around and tell us what you see.

It's not as dark as it was. I don't feel as bad as I did.

Your shame is entirely self-inflicted. You'll be welcomed with open arms when you get to the light.

I do see a lighter area over there.

The easiest thing to do is simply quickly go there. That's all it takes. [Gone.]

T At least three people were waiting for her. Someone hugged her.

P Sounds like it was a difficult life.

◊ ◊ ◊

T I feel really queasy. Someone is here. Another woman.

C We welcome you here. Why do you choose to come and visit us?

T *I didn't choose to be here. I just seem to have turned up. I haven't seen anyone else for a long time. It's odd. Do I need to be worried about you people?*

P No, we're harmless. Open your heart and feel our energy. Can you see your physical body?

No.

What does that tell you?

It's a bit weird! Am I dreaming?

No, you've passed away. You're not alive and in physical form any more. What's the last thing you remember?

T She killed someone else as well. Husband.

C How did you die?

There was a court case. I died in prison.

You must have been very lonely there. Are there any loved ones you could look for now?

My daughter.

What year did they put you in prison?

1977, in NZ.

The other inmates ganged up on her.

Can you call your mother to come for you?

T Gone. Her mother came straight away. She thought her mum wouldn't want to see her, but she called anyway.

R It's like someone saw the previous lady with the similar circumstances, saw we helped her, and pushed this lady forward too.

◊ ◊ ◊

T My head got turned to the left. A man. He feels very calm and self-contained. He committed suicide. *I'd had enough of life. Took pills.*

P Is there an inability to express pain?

I'm not in any pain. Back then, yes, I was. I was unhappy. I'm fine now. Resigned, but not in a bad way. This is better than what I had before.

Why are you still here?

What else is there?

Don't you know about what lies beyond death?

I did commit suicide. And I'm not in hell, so maybe this is it. This is okay.

That implies you had religious instruction about heaven and hell?

Yes.

What religion?

As a child. Protestant, not Catholic.

What's your expectation now?

Just this, I suppose.

So if not hell, then what?

Well, I'm in no pain. I'm emotionless.

Bored?

Well, yes, I guess. But it's still better than what I had.

You seem curiously passive about the alternative. If hell hasn't manifested, where is heaven? Surely you have some curiosity?

Yes, but I committed suicide.

So?

Surely I don't deserve to go to heaven.

Why not?

Because it's a bad thing to do.

Who says?

Church people.

From our perspective it's just another way out of a life.

I guess I'm open to alternatives.

Heaven is a possibility.

You mean I could have a happy life?

Why not? In fact, many more. Have you heard of rebirth into another body?

I thought that was hocus pocus.

In this realm it's not. How would you feel about another life?

I'd like to have a happy life. You're not just the devil come to trick me or something?

Do I look or feel devilish?

No.

Perhaps you could consider the possibility with hope for pleasure, peace and love, and clarification about your options.

I'd like to be loved.

You already are.

I've never felt it before.

Take a sip from what we can offer you and consider it multiplied many times. That's your immediate future.

I've got nothing to lose, have I?

Precisely. Is your mother in spirit? Ask her to come for you.

My parents both died when I was very young. Is that really them? She looks pleased to see me.

[Gone.]

◊ ◊ ◊

T I've got a wary feeling that's not mine.

P I felt I needed to look far over the horizon. Is that connected? I'm getting male, nearly naked, tall, powerfully built, a hunter or tribesman. Doesn't feel recent. He seems comfortable to be with our group. He's got his back to us and is looking at the horizon.

T Yes, I'm seeing him from behind. I was admiring his butt!

C I'm getting he's from a long, long time ago. Maybe Ice Age?

P They would have worn more. He's white skinned, tanned.

C *So now you've observed me, why am I here?*

P Please tell us something about yourself.

I'm just me. What do you want to know?

What is your family like?

I haven't seen my family for ages.

What sort of shelter do you live in?

I've just been wandering for a long, long time.

I understand that, but before.

Animal skins and sticks and poles.

You do realise you're dead?

I realise I'm not embodied, yes.

Is there a name for your culture or your tribe?

My name is White Wolf.

Do you understand the countries of the world?

I know the nature of the country I come from: mountains and valleys and rivers and forest.

Why have you not returned to the light long since?

I'm a guardian.

Guarding what?

Guarding those I left behind, watching over them. It's my duty.

Did you not understand there's a time limit to such duty?

No.

How many summers have you seen?

Over three hundred.

Did you observe changes in the ways of those who you guarded?

Yes.

Did you understand those changes?

No. I stay with them. They're my people.

Do they know of your presence?

Some do.

Did they tell you of the changes in your culture?

Some have.

Then you understand that your culture is radically altered.

Yes. I still must stay I believe.

Who requested you to accept that duty?

My father.

Where is he now?

I suppose I've taken his place. So I'm waiting for someone to take my place.

Can you consider that that role is no longer required?

Then what is to become of me?

What are your myths about destiny after death?

I become a watcher and someone replaces me. I don't know the next step.

Consider that those who might have come after you have not been taught these things.

I believe I was to be called to a home place and I haven't heard the call so I haven't gone. Do you think they've forgotten to call me and left me here? Where are my ancestors?

I think your belief that a role hasn't ended has prevented you from hearing any other call. If you open your awareness beyond this small location, what do you see?

A very strong bright moonlight over the mountains.

You are not in the physical world any more..

The moonlight is very warm and I feel drawn towards it.

The best thing you can do is allow yourself to be drawn. Expect to find those who would take you further. Your duty is done. You have performed your service well. We offer our thanks and bid you farewell.

P Why do I feel that he's not gone?

C He hasn't. He's stuck, pinned.

P Why?

T Is it just expectation? I feel like he feels he'd be letting his people down if he abandons his post.

C He has to be invited by some great person to leave.

P Does he know the name Wakantanka?

C Yes.

P Ask Wakantanka what would he have you do now.

C That's it. He's been invited. You can't go unless you're invited.
[Gone.]

C He had a spear through him. That's how he died. He's ashamed that he wasn't strong enough, felt he shouldn't have died. He wanted to stay around to make up for getting himself killed.

◊ ◊ ◊

C I have someone else. I'm feeling really, really furious, and I don't think that's me!

R Welcome. How may we be of service to you?

C *What on earth do think you could possibly do to be of service to me!*

I don't know. That's why we asked!

This is not where I'm supposed to be. I was driving along and now I'm late for an appointment. What the hell am I doing here? I'm a very busy, VERY important man. It's most inconvenient that I'm in this bizarre place. I've got to be somewhere. Why are we fiddle-faddling around here?

It must be very frustrating for you.

Absolutely right! So where am I and how can I get to my meeting? I'm holding up a very important meeting!

Unfortunately, you won't be able to get to the meeting.

I'm going to the meeting!

It may come as a surprise, but you've passed over to the other side.

Well, get my chauffeur to get me on the right side of town.

You sound like a person who's pretty straight, so I'll put it to you straight. You've died.

Right.

Can you see your body?

Well … it doesn't seem to be here at the moment.

What country are you from?

America.

And what year is it?

1974. Stupid question.

We're in the year 2014.

Okay, what's happened? It's some joke, some kind of nonsense!

K What did you do that was so important?

Build skyscrapers. People are waiting for me. This is ridiculous.

Maybe you need to go to the top floor!

This is part of the joke is it?

There's probably a big surprise waiting for you at the top.

Oh yeah, right.

Get in the elevator and go up.

Okay, I'll play along. Why can I see my daughter? She died aged four.

Because you've gone up to the very top level.

Oh, my god!

[Gone.]

C He wasn't happy. Convinced it was all a prank!

T He had a heart attack.

C There's something else. It isn't finished.

T I think his wife is here too. I feel a little downtrodden. She doesn't want to go where he went.

C Yes, that's the question she's asking: *Do I still have to be married to him if I go there too?* No, you're free now.

[Gone.]

R If he died forty years ago, she could have died of natural causes in that time.

◊ ◊ ◊

T I feel someone else here. Male. He's wondering why he's here.

C Welcome. How can we help you?

I've watched what you have been doing this evening.

P We're a group of friends who assemble to help people who are confused about what happens to them after they die.

I've served as a priest my whole life, and never have I seen such a demonstration of the power of love.

C Thank you. Have you found the light yourself?

I have been speaking of it my whole life, but apparently not believing it, because no such thing has happened to me. I feel a charlatan, that I've been speaking of the love and light available to my flock.

You are no charlatan.

But I was taught to tell them of sin and bad and wrong, and I caused more fear than love. Yet they were looking to me for guidance into the next life. I feel I was the one blaspheming and telling them they had to be better, pray more, yet I was the one who was so in darkness rather than light.

So take this as a lesson.

What of all the people who I turned against the light? What did I do to them by preaching fear and damnation and hell and evil and burning? What did I do to the people who trusted me for salvation or a way to it, yet all I taught them was hell and brimstone, their shortcomings and sins.

P They had choice whether to listen and believe and apply it.

So have I not condemned all those who listened to me to darkness?

No, because they had choice. Don't condemn yourself. You did as you were trained and according the love you felt. Mistakes are just mistakes, things we learn from to reach to a more knowledgable place.

But who forgives me for what I –

No forgiveness is necessary.

But I believe it, I taught it. I need to be forgiven for the sin of turning people away from the light. I've seen your demonstration of the light. It never occurred to me to teach that. I taught the opposite.

R What's your belief around forgiveness?

Because of what I taught I can now see that I was potentially wrong in what I taught, though I believed it was right and true. You're saying that I'm not wrong?

C Not if you believe in yourself. There is no right or wrong. There's a new journey for you, of your choosing.

P Can you forgive yourself? That's the only requirement. Ask for the grace and it will be yours. Use that grace to forgive yourself and come to peace. You won't be judged.

If it is God's will that I be accepted as I am, then so be it.

Then it will be so.

Bless you all for leading me to this.

C We've heard your confession and our love for you has not changed. Take this into your heart and go to the light. They're waiting.

[Gone.]

Rescues and an endorsement

T I have someone on my left.

P Welcome. It feels like they're checking us out. [Addressing the visitor.] Our purpose is to assist those who come in peace and seek help.

T *I don't need help.* Feels suspicious.

P Please share your circumstances with us.

I don't really know how I got here.

What's the last thing you remember?

That feels like a trick question. I can't remember anything. That's strange. I don't notice anybody physically present.

Are you aware you're in your spirit nature and not your body?

Huh?

Examine the body through which you're speaking. Is it yours?

No.

So something has changed.

Is this a dream?

No. We think you're dead now.

Laughs uncomfortably.

Had you noticed?

Crap!

Were you male or female?

Male.

So you don't belong in this female body. Do you know where you belong now?

Yes, I do. I just didn't realise this is where I was.

Where have you been?

Just here.

What year do you think it is?

I died in the 1970's. I guess I've been stuck here all that time. I had no idea.

Well, you'll have been in a grave, not knowing where to go.

I don't remember anything before seeing you guys.

I invite you to expand your awareness, to understand your condition, to recognise that the life you've been living ended some forty years ago. What do you understand as being your next destination?

I do know about the light. I do know that.

Then look for it. What do you see? Look around you.

But why didn't it come to me sooner?

Maybe you didn't realise you were dead, therefore it couldn't. You need to be conscious of these things. How did you die? Do you remember how old you were?

In my thirties. I died in an accident.

When you look around you what do you see?

There's light seeping under a door over there. It's beautiful.

Go to it. We wish you well. Expect to find there people who will show you what to do next.

[Gone.]

T When the door opened I got a little buzz in the top right side of my head.

C I got that he was drunk, that's why he didn't remember the accident. It numbed the senses.

R I got really hot.

K I had restless legs.

◊ ◊ ◊

T Queasy. I sense the presence of more than one person. [There were actually forty-eight.]

R Welcome to our group. How can we be of service to you?

T There's a feeling of agitation, worry, fear.

R Fear of ... ?

Someone.

Someone hunting them, after them when they were alive? Are

you aware that you're now in spirit, and dead? You no longer need to fear anyone you feared before.

Won't they be here, too?

Perhaps, but they are unable to harm you. You no longer have physical bodies. Do you understand that?

Yes.

Are you aware of the next stage in your transition?

It feels better already just knowing that actually we're safe.

Those that have gone before you are waiting to welcome you and take you to the next stage.

I'm getting they were in a building set on fire. Deliberately.

What year?

1828. In New Zealand. Gisborne.

It's now 2014. If you choose to do so, you can move on now to the next stage.

We're ready.

When you look around, what do you see?

Our elders are waiting for us.

Go to them.

[Gone.]

T Māori. As they were going they forgave whoever it was.

◊ ◊ ◊

T I have a girl with me. Not spirit, not someone who wants help. There's green all around, like bush. She's ten years old, dressed in animal skins. It's a prehistoric feel and look.

What's her demeanour? How does she feel?

Calm. Just there, a presence. She doesn't want anything from me.

Does she understand her condition?

She's not a spirit needing moved on. It's a message for me.

Is this you at another time, an associate, a child of yours?

No connection.

Image the world and find her location. What's the country?

I get a continent. South America.

What's her colour?

White, blond.

Does she acknowledge you? I wonder if this is a sustained, structured, safe continuance of her surroundings, which is actually false but brings her comfort.

I get a yes to that.

So this fixed location has provided stability, continuity. Though it feels comfortable and she feels at peace, it's a temporary location. She needs to move on.

I get a yes.

I invite her to wake up to her true nature and her true condition, and recognise she's been in a holding pattern for a very long time. Now she's been brought to our attention it's an opportunity to find her way to her true home in spirit. We can help her. Does she acknowledge that?

Yes.

So invite her to expand her awareness beyond her familiar, safe but false surroundings, to take down those walls surrounding her perception and find her next opportunity.

[Gone.]

She went really quickly. Something Peter said triggered sudden understanding.

P It's a good example of how a person can construct a complete environment out of astral matter. It's temporary parking.

◊ ◊ ◊

P I have an image of a group of people walking up a narrow, unformed road. Military.

T They were on reconnaissance. They were looking all around, but there was a bomb. A booby trap.

P Can one person come forward as a representative?

T *We feel like we're stuck here. What if there's another bomb? We're kind of scared to move.*

C You're now in spirit, not physical form, so there's no fear.

But if we carry on up that path there might be another bomb.

You need to acknowledge that you are no longer alive in physical form. Do you know what this means to you?

No.

You have all died. You're no longer in human form. You do know what death is, don't you?

Yes.

There are ones amongst you that believe in angels; step forward and be representative. Trust that we're here; you've been drawn to us because we are the light. We are a portal for you to pass through. Hold hands, and we'll help you to move on to the beautiful light you see before you. Can you see it?

We're being lifted. It's a bit weird. It's like we held hands and a couple of the guys there, they turned into angels or something, and they're just taking us all. So I guess we're going.

[*All seventeen gone.*]

T Robin and I had a lot of pressure on our heads, from the bomb. Heads blown off?

◊ ◊ ◊

T Someone else is here.

P I'm slowly rocking, as if on a boat. There's the feeling of a sea swell. Not rough, steady.

T I get a one-person boat. It's a female.

P I have an image of being between headlands, in sight of land, but a substantial stretch of water. Going round the headland on the east coast.

I'm getting that she didn't drown. There was a storm and she hit her head.

Does she know she's dead?

No, but she's fairly content because she's still just out on the sea where she loves it.

Sustaining the imagery.

She's used to being on her own.

I think she needs to look beyond her self-sustained bubble of reality; throw down the walls, see where she is and what her options are. It's a comforting illusion that she's constructed.

I guess maybe it's time to move on, go back to people who love me.

Good idea. Are you ready now?

Sure.

Use our loving awareness as a springboard to send you on to the light. Gone?

T Yes. Her mother and some other family members were there waiting for her. It felt like a one-person boat. I felt like I was shifting the sail from side to side.

P Tacking. The storm was much worse than she expected. I have a strange visualisation of a tall male trying to climb up something, contorting himself around trying to reach and climb, reach and climb. A little bit frantic. In your direction, Karen. Are you receiving any of these impressions?

K No. But I had really sore lower arms and hands.

P Try reach to him. Feel his condition.

It's very black, like a hole. Dizzy.

If he fell you might feel like that.

The right side of his head is sore. [*Trisha saw him falling down a hole, like he'd been abseiling.*] There's a hole or a cave. Rocks.

[*At this point Peter explained to the visitor that he had died and tried talking him up and out. But he was very resistant, being convinced there was no way out. Did he have unfinished business, a sense of shame?*]

Maybe he deserves it.

That's ultimately untrue. Besides his life is over. He's overdue to move on to the next stage of his life.

[*Gone.*]

I felt a fear of being buried alive.

C It was a deep tomb.

T I had a flash of something else while that was going on. A wedding party. Something happened to the groom on the way to the wedding, and they're still waiting for him. The groom died on the way to the wedding, but they don't seem to know that. Seven years after the wedding the wedding party were all dead. Yet they're still waiting for the groom. How bizarre.

P What country?

T America. The groom has already gone to the light.

So what happened to the wedding party? Why are they still waiting for him?

It's not the bride. It's three bridesmaids! The bride is still alive.

Perhaps just let them know they are waiting in vain? Ask them to call for the groom. Perhaps he'll come and collect them.

They all had affairs with him. They all died in separate circumstances within seven years of him dying. He just whistled for them. Like, I'm up here! They're going. He's a lucky guy.

Charismatic fellow!

◊ ◊ ◊

P [Channelling his guides.] *We come to offer feedback for the purpose of further directing this well-functioning group. A steady stream of these individuals, small groups, and occasionally larger groups, will continue to be brought here for your processing. You are very, very good at it. Your skill will not be wasted, given it has taken years to accrue.*

These exercises, in some instances severe, were specifically devised to test you. You have survived all manner of temptations that could have brought you into error. You have also avoided rigid doctrines and escape mechanisms of one sort or another, which could have taken you far away from the simple and easy processing of individuals who are themselves sometimes very complicated. This is not to mention the broad varieties of identities brought into your domain to test both your capabilities and your willingness to accept perceptions at face value—even when that face value was deliberately falsified to create a more difficult test. You have passed all tests. We have confidence in your capacities now.

It is for this purpose that the group has been supported these many years. Your solidity of knowledge and steadiness of purpose can now be built on as new, less experienced people arrive into the group. Would you be willing to welcome inexperienced newcomers, and greet and counsel them with love, as they develop their own natural capacities in a simple, easy, uninflated way? And will you offer love to those who are brought to you that they may ascend onwards?

All said yes.

Then it shall be done. We will provide you with an incremental series of opportunities, involving other interested individuals and parties. These procedures need not be elevated into the divine, but may be understood as a simple consequence of being human.

We acknowledge your undoubted competence. You are now ready. Your teaching capabilities will be utilised to achieve the best outcome for all who are shepherded into your presence. For this is not done without help, but rather involves an expansive network, of which you are now part on the fully conscious level. We celebrate this with you, and now leave you in peace.

An alien encounter

The session began with three soul rescues. The first was of a woman who died after being beaten and was hiding, too scared to come out in case the man who hurt her was still around. She went into the light after seeing her parents. The second was a woman who died in the 1960s and had taken refuge in her memories. She saw a door and went through it. The third was a man who died of illness away from home and was lost, not knowing what to do. He was encouraged to call out to his former wife, saw her, and left. The following then occurred.

    T Something's up there. Something to my right, looking down. I said in my head, "Is there anyone else we can help?" and I got this feeling like they thought that was the strangest thing they'd ever heard!

    Cr The voice that was talking to you, who do you feel it was?

    T I just felt they were looking at me. It didn't feel uncomfortable. I'm sure they think I'm an upstart, wondering, *What's she doing now!*

    P Put your attention back there. Check it out, see what you get.

    T They're still there. Watching, curious.

    P What's their status? Are they between lives?

    M No.

    P Are they human?

    T No.

    P I invite them to share themselves with us as an opportunity to learn about a non-human species. *[No response.]* I seem to be getting some information about a non-Earth environment. It's not clear.

    T All I'm getting is they're curious why I'd want to help people.

    P Ask them what they know of love. Is that a familiar concept?

    T No, they don't seem to know what love is.

P This is very interesting.

T They saw our glow, were drawn by it, and are curious.

P *[Addressing the entity.]* The basis on which we relate to one another is on the core level. It's an attraction based on a loving nature, a desire to nurture, and a willingness to encourage development of any identity, whatever its nature. Is this a motivation you experience?

No.

In that case, what is the basis for your actions?

Selfishness.

In other words, looking for advantage?

Yes. They think we are too idealistic.

In what way would you describe the basis on which you exist?

Independently, not working in a group like this.

B How often have you communicated with humans on Earth?

This is the first time.

B Do you have any questions you'd like to ask us?

What you're doing will be your downfall.

P Thank you for that prognosis, but we prefer to think otherwise. How did you arrive here?

I was drawn by your light.

Are you curious how it is that we can converse with you?

Yes.

What are your perceptions about that?

It's not something I've experienced before.

How do you experience our communication? Is it purely a mental phenomenon, or is there some mechanism or technique required?

Some other technique.

Is that something you can describe, or not?

T My head got turned to the left, like he was looking over there. I think another spirit's there. He's watching to see how we deal with this.

P It's an important educational moment for us all. How is it this identity can understand our language without organs of hearing? How is it we can communicate using concepts you understand?

I've never experienced it before. I just know that I can understand you.

Speaking for myself, I'm delighted to make your acquaintance. Much information can flow in such opportunities as these. Are there any observations you wish to make?

T We're more enlightened than he thought humans were. Interestingly, he started right up there and to the right, but now he's down here.

B He's melding with us. Can you identify yourself to us, as you haven't been here before. Can you tell us your planet and name?

T When I ask if he can tell us what planet he's from I get a yes.

P Is it within this universe?

T No.

B I got that too. I feel they've come a long way.

P We're delighted to make your acquaintance. I don't think we've met somebody from an entirely different universe.

T He's sitting cross-legged right among us now. When I ask if he would like to visit us again I get a yes.

B He has a new respect for us. He's acknowledging us as like a council. He doesn't see us as mere mortals.

P Does that mean that he's responding to the purely spiritual aspect of us, and not so much to the physical manifestation?

B Yes.

P Good. How can it possibly be that he is ignorant of love?

B I feel it's the way his planet was formed. It was like they were dumped there, and they have not learnt this.

T I get a yes to that.

P So it's not a cooperative physical species that would require loving relationships, not a social species but a solitary species?

T Solitary, yes.

P There are solitary species on this planet too, so it's not unknown. So as we are an embodied and social species, that probably means that we elevate the factor of loving nature in a way that would be simply irrelevant to a solitary species.

B He's acknowledging our love energy.

P I get a curious sensation in the middle of my chest saying that.

T When you said that, Craig, I thought, I'm going to consciously send him more love. I did and I felt I was sending him away, like he was backing away from it.

B But not afraid.

P What do you think was the motivation for backing away? Simply unfamiliarity? Or discomfort?

T He's just never experienced it.

B Can you tell us why you've chosen to leave the place where you were and come so far into the unknown?

We're sent out to travel. I saw your light. This golden light attracted me.

P Have you encountered anything similar to that previously?

No.

How many other universes or star systems have you visited?

Four universes.

What are your intentions in terms of staying present in proximity to this planet? And who sent you?

I'll stay here for a while.

B You judged yourself selfish. How did the other universes find you when you communicated with them? Were you welcome?

No.

P Is any part of your role to do with a process of surveying?

Yes.

So is part of your role to sample the condition and status of life in various locations?

Yes.

What do you do with the information?

I take it all back home.

B So you are here to learn?

Yes.

With what intention?

To improve our planet.

Why?

People aren't happy.

When you say people, what do you mean?

I sensed population, life-force.

Is it a relatively young planet?

Yes.

Are you looking for ideas to contribute to species diversity on your planet?

T   He's gone.

P   I'd like to communicate with the supervisory identity he was aware of, that you perceived. Is communication available through you?

T   *Yes.*

P   *[To the supervising identity.]* Please introduce yourself and provide a comprehensive explanation of everything that it's appropriate for us to know about that identity and yourself, if you would be so kind.

I'm getting that he'd like to speak through someone else, but it's not someone who's here. At least, I get a no to each of us.

Is it feasible to do so at a different time?

Yes.

Then you'd be most welcome to contribute another time and to join us then. We feel that we have the opportunity to learn a considerable amount through this interaction, so please find a way if you may.

[Gone.]

P   How did it feel to be talking to an alien?

Fine.

There's a whole lot of unanswered questions here.

At the end I really felt like I was really open to him speaking through me, but it just wasn't going to happen.

B   Same. I was asking. He could have but chose not to. I think he was astounded at our power, our abilities.

P   Our communicative abilities?

B   Not being afraid. It's like it we were, say, kings, and a subordinate came to talk respectfully. He had that respect for us in his energy.

P   Humans are very highly regarded because it's a tough place!

B It was quite something to acknowledge that while it was going on. It was like I felt a higher being than I normally feel.

T There was no bad feeling at all, just curiosity.

P What about willingness to exploit?

T No, it literally just felt like he wanted to watch and take it all in, not that he was using us in any way. He just didn't understand the concept of helping someone else.

P If you're a solitary species, sure, why would you want to help anyone else? It isn't built into your system, like it is ours.

B It would have been interesting to know his ranking, his role.

P On his world, you mean?

B I think on his planet there was a governing role controlling the planet, totally opposite to our free will. That's what I got. Perhaps that wasn't working. Maybe that's why he's looking for new ideas.

R Just part of the big experiment.

P The supervisory element that you spotted—was that the feeling that you got, that there was an organiser?

T When you said that, I got a yes.

P Right at the beginning I sensed someone really big over there, but I didn't stay connected with it at all.

T I didn't get that until the first guy had gone.

P It's normal to have that class of identity with us, just to make sure everything goes well. To run the show, educate us, foster these interactions, and usher through the string of identities that need intervention. It's a while since we've connected with that level. It's hard to get a feel for it because it's not usually obvious.

T We need the extra presence for the energy.

P The energy goes up according to square of the participants. It's a geometric/arithmetic thing.

T Someone else is here.

R Our watcher is still here. Or he's come back on the right again.

P Is there something that could function as a name, an identifier?

T I get a yes to that. But I'm not seeing anything.

P I presume you have returned to continue the observation role?

Yes.

P I think we have other business. You're welcome to observe.

R I get Timothy as an identifier. Is that a suitable name?

T I get that that's not his name, but a name we can use for him. Let's get back to business. Is there anybody out there who needs our help? I got a real big shiver. I felt like maybe it was him going: *Here we go again—helping and love!* He's perplexed by our desire to help people.

P It might be the case. As a species we forget our spiritual nature. It might be that he's a species that doesn't forget, therefore the idea that you need to remind somebody just doesn't exist.

◊ ◊ ◊

The following exchange took place a week later. It includes a discussion of concepts explained in the Appendices.

T There's someone on my left. I feel my eyes moving around a lot, so I think they're curious about us and why they're here.

P Let's collectively welcome them, whoever they are. Is it Timothy?

T Yes, it is. *[Laughs.]* He's checking you out, Richard!

R I'm afraid he'll be disappointed!

T He's looking at Peter now. *Did you invite me here?*

P It seems so. I was advised you would be present. So I didn't consciously invite you, but you're most welcome.

You are most welcome.

Having been forewarned of your likely return this evening, one of us not physically present has prepared some questions. Perhaps we could pose these questions to you. Is that okay?

Yes.

On your last visit with us you said that you came from a planet from a different universe. Is that correct?

Yes.

How do you interact on your planet?

It's a knowing.

Do you occupy bodies that move on some part of the planet?

Yes.

What aspect of the planet do you move in?

In the air.

Do you float? Move rapidly?

Yes.

Can you describe the body type in relation to the creatures that inhabit the air of this planet?

It's not the same.

How similar is the composition of the atmosphere of your planet?

It's very similar.

How do you suspend the bodies of the beings you inhabit in the air?

We use our minds.

Are the bodies adapted for flight through that atmosphere?

No, it's purely mind.

So they levitate through mind control. Very interesting. Do you have specific tasks?

T He's fixated on Carolyn and expects the interpretation to come from her.

P Okay. When you're ready, Carolyn.

C *Our community—*

P Can we go back one step, because last time you said that you lived as solitary individuals.

But you asked about our tasks, and our tasks require cooperation. We may be solitary, but for us all to survive we have to collaborate.

How do the dimensions compare between your planet and Earth?

Ten times bigger.

Is it a solid planet, or a gas planet?

Solid.

So it's similar in general composition to this planet?

Yes.

Why are you associated with a planet if you are purely spiritual?

C Can I just go back. The comment about aloneness, it's regarding procreation. *We don't need a mate to procreate. Your question was in relation to relationships. So we are alone in the sense that we believe the ques-*

*tion asked last week was about relationships with others. On this planet you
need relationships to procreate. Because we don't do that, in that sense we are
alone. Obviously we still have to communicate, corroborate, cohabitate.*

If you are not sexually segregated, how do you procreate?

*We choose to move on, and others move into the environment. So we
move out of this space on to something else and others will come in. We don't
have to regenerate ourselves.*

What is your life span in terms of earthly revolutions?

Eighty years.

Eighty Earth years?

Yes. We don't age. In your terms that's the length of time we spend there.

R What are your bodies? Are they bodies of light or energy?

*Energy bodies. Our bodies aren't drawn from organic material, so it's not
a body as you understand it.*

C I see this sphere-ish sort of shape. Almost like jelly fish but solid.
They are energy but like clear jelly fish. Huge sensitivity around them.

P In one visit to a much higher level I saw an organism similar to
what you describe. I attributed it to the non-physical aspect of a human.

Yes.

Are you saying that in our natures we are no different from you?

We are humans without bodies. Similar to humanity, without bodies.

Why do you associate with that planet if you need no physical
sustenance from it?

Magic is sustenance.

Can you explain that?

*It allows us to commune with each other, in a space that is comfortable
cohabiting space. We are there for a period of time before going on to embodiment again somewhere else. So it isn't an embodiment planet. It's a space
where we are communal, but not necessarily having to take on a body.*

Why associate with a planet if you are purely spiritual? You're
saying for social reasons. Does that mean it's a suitable environment
within which to prepare for embodiment elsewhere?

C The thing I get is there's no emotion. When you're embodied
and communing, there's everything that goes on from previous issues.

That planet is a place to commune peacefully without the previous interactions we have when we're embodied. I want to emphasise the peacefulness of it. So they're communing with others, but with a totally clean slate.

P You have no bodies as we do, therefore you have no human emotions and developing personalities with the potential for conflict.

No personalities.

Only what we call the higher spiritual emotions and qualities.

Yes.

What does that association give them for their evolution?

C I see groups of them getting together, almost little globules of them all joining. They seem to be part of a group, forming little groups.

R Is this preparatory to the next stage of their evolution?

C It's almost like they're one. They split up again back into their ten. Or do they leave there in their group of ten? They find those who harmonise with them.

P So it's coordination?

Yes, they leave there. They join together. It's like a soul group.

And does such a group have a common destination, into a species of some kind somewhere?

I'm just going to ask them to try and tell me in words instead of showing me in pictures.

Pictures are good. Just describe them as best you can, as they come to you. What are you seeing? Can you describe it?

I don't understand it, but I see the group of ten in a ball.

So it's a kind of clump or cluster?

Yes. It's just rolling around, joining other clusters of balls all together into this huge ... probably twenty to thirty balls. They're all together in a big ball.

Why are they doing that?

A nest.

Is this the reaggregation process, reforming groups that were one?

That feels right.

So are these individuals who have completed their round of physical incarnations?

Yes. But there are other balls, other clumps. They're floating too.
There's all these clumps of ten balls. Like Christmas decorations!

Is it exactly ten, or about ten?

It's ten.

Why ten?

The ten that were in the first ball have joined a clump. There are
incomplete clumps, waiting for the other groups of ten to join them.
They have more than ten, more like twenty, all joining into their
clump.

So would it be appropriate to describe these as fragments of a
node of Dao-conciousness, which is in the process of reassembling?

Yes. There's lots of incomplete clumps waiting for others to join.

So those are individual identities who have completed their
round of physical lives?

Yes.

So you are being shown a representative image of the way in
which personalities accumulate at the end of a life to form a higher
self?

Imagine the beautiful light that you bounce off a crystal. It's like
that light is almost sparkling. There's so much light around these
clumps. It's really powerful. Beautiful.

Okay, I'll proceed with the questions otherwise we'll never get
through them. Why is this identity travelling through universes?

To introduce himself to embodied people, to pass on information.

What are you looking for? Individuals like us?

Yes, whoever will listen.

Is this a random search?

No, it's planned.

By what are you being directed in that plan?

A really big clump. And it's a gold colour, really gold.

When you say really big, what do you mean?

It's umm ... a mothership!

Who do you report back to?

I just see this big gold ship.

Are you fragments of a node of Dao-consciousness the way we are?

Yes.

Do you eventually reintegrate on a higher spiritual level like we do?

I don't.

In what way are you different from that?

I just get the word servant.

What does that mean?

It is my job to move around.

Last week there appeared to Trisha's awareness a separate individual apparently acting as observer or guide. What is that?

T I've got observer.

P Why is observation appropriate?

To oversee.

Is this a developmental task, an end goal?

Yes.

So the guide is a supervisor?

Yes.

Is this an engineered meeting?

Yes.

For whose benefit?

This group.

If this alien who has travelled from another universe hasn't previously met entities like this group, why has this meeting occurred?

It's time to start meeting with groups such as this on this planet.

Have similar groups been met on different planets?

Yes. Raising awareness.

Why, and of what?

Your curiosity.

T My feeling about the observer is there's absolutely no judgement. It's not checking up on Timothy or anything like that. He's just here. Also we can put any questions. There's nothing Timothy won't answer.

R He mentioned that the reason for making contact was that it was time that groups like us knew about the existence of their group. Why do they want us to know about them?

It's not that it is time, but that there is opportunity. So we're just going to groups where opportunity is ready. It's not that we've got to go and visit everybody. You're ready to know.

R Right. But why would they want us to know?

To start a dialogue.

For what purpose?

Raising awareness.

P So this is raising awareness within today's population?

I just get that it's important.

I take it this is not the only time in the history of this planet that it's been considered important to transfer this awareness?

No.

Can you describe other times when similar contact has been made?

Atlantis.

I have no idea when or where Atlantis was. When else?

I'm not getting any other times.

Can you transfer information into this recipient regarding the time period and location of what you're identifying as Atlantis?

I just got Barbados.

R How many Earth years ago was it?

3000.

R Last week he said that our association, our helping each other, would be our downfall. I'd like to know what was meant by that.

You must help yourselves. You don't have a responsibility to assist anybody else, to reduce or give away your capacity, disempower yourselves.

P Because everybody is ultimately responsible for themselves. Which is interesting, because it says that this desire to help may be largely from the social animal aspect.

C Yes, there's the personality help, there's a charity help, and then there's the help that you're doing with each other, which is good. So helping each other grow is good, as opposed to disempowering yourself by helping someone else.

P Mutual support is equality, rather than ...

C In relationship to the comment, *Helping will be your downfall,* I see people toppling because they've been pulled by others. Pulled down by this wonderful spiritual helping of others, being charitable.

P This is really interesting because caritas is a fundamental principle of Christianity, a core value.

C But you can't help others unless you are strong yourself. So keep your strength and offer it when—

You're strong?

Yes. Don't form co-dependent groups.

I would request any information which has not been gleaned in this session to be suggested to us at a future time, and I invite Timothy to return on every occasion when your contribution can assist us. Is this feasible; is it available?

Yes, very much so.

Is there a time frame within which this can occur?

Time irrelevant. It's available to generations of you.

Excellent. I'd like to draw this session to a close and give thanks for your contribution and communication here. We look forward to communicating again.

It will be done.

R I'm delighted to have this contact. I find it extremely interesting.

You're welcome.

[Gone.]

P I'm really interested in why it might have been appropriate for the focus to transfer to Carolyn from you, Trisha.

T Because I don't have the words. I felt him looking around and thinking, "She'll do!" I felt a shift when Carolyn started talking. Prior to that I could feel him, then he was gone. I didn't get any of the pictures Carolyn saw.

C I felt completely and utterly unworthy.

P Did you!

C She's better than me, so why was I doing it?

P It's a really good question.

C I haven't done this for ages, so I was asking, why me? That got in the way a lot. I didn't prepare myself for tonight.

P I'm curious, Trisha, why you felt you don't have the words?

T It's interesting. I'm laughing at Carolyn saying she's not good enough, because I'm like, "Here, Carolyn, take this because I can't do it!" If you ask me specific questions, with yes/no questions, I can answer them. But I don't get flowing words. I was muscle-testing, getting what I thought was the answer, then double-checking.

C I'd like to do what Peter does. He asks questions and answers them, and it comes out in words. But I don't get words, I get pictures. Then I don't know what to look for. The little jellyfish clumps floating around, I had to watch and see what they did. Then there was this big thing above them that I called the mothership. I think the word mothership was my interpretation, not his naming. The feeling of Atlantis was my feeling of an ancient civilisation. It could have been Egypt, but it was the word that my head picked out to interpret the civilisation I saw. It's really hard because it was my interpretation. I don't want anyone to take it literally.

P What you're raising is everybody's dilemma: how to be the clear big pipe this stuff can pour through, without interpretation. That's almost impossible, because perception itself involves an interpretation. Translation into words is an interpretation. It's a problem.

The flower tickler

T Someone is here.

P Welcome. Why are you here?

T *I'm just watching.*

P And what do you see when you watch?

I see you people.

What do we look like to you?

Unusual.

In what way?

Most people don't do what you're doing.

What is it you think we're doing?

Being open to what's out there.

We certainly try to do that. You're out there. Who are you?

I'm not sure I should tell you!

Why not? I think you can tell us anything.

[Laughing.] The feeling is cheeky. I feel giggly. *[More laughing.]*

So who brought you here? I suspect you didn't come on your own.

[More giggling.] I don't want to tell you my secrets.

Oh, it's a secret?

Yes!

Have you been having fun?

Yes!

Tell us about what sort of fun? Are you having a good time?

[Laughs, claps hands.]

T He doesn't want to say. I know, but he doesn't want to say.

P So why are you here? Have you had enough of the mischief?

Awwww. I suppose.

Who have you been playing with?

He's okay to tell you now. Mica brought him.

[An elemental, to which they gave the name Mica, had first appeared to Trisha several weeks earlier. Mica had previously been in communication with Trisha's paternal grandfather, as well as with earlier individuals on that side of the family. This communication was being continued through Trisha.]

P Well, thank you, Mica. This seems like a service. Someone who perhaps doesn't quite want to be here!

T Yes, it feels like Mica wanted to let him experience something different, something new. He hadn't experienced people like us before doing this, and he thinks it's really funny. Like, *Ha ha, look at them! What are they doing? Weird!*

So who have we here in spirit? Where has he been, what has he been doing, and on what kind of level?

He feels gnome-like to me. I'm thinking garden gnome. When he was giggling I felt short and fat. I get a yes to that.

Something to do with the earth?

Yes, to do with gardens.

What is his role? Does he support something? Is he here for his benefit, or ours, or both?

All of our benefits.

Good. How can we help then?

I see lots of colour. It's to do with flowers, blooms.

A particular species of flower, or all flowers in general? Flowers are about sexual propagation of plants. Does he have some role in relation to that?

Yes.

What?

T I keep getting ... but it sounds either weird or slightly perverse. Tickling the flowers!

P That's interesting. That might stimulate development, readiness for the pollination process.

I'm making the flowers happy!

Is that a kind of love for them?

Yes.

Does that make them breed better?

It just makes them happy.

That's good. Is that what you're there for, or do you do other things?

I just make the flowers happy. I guess they like that. I'm very good at it.

I expect so. What kinds of flowers? Where are they?

Everywhere.

Everywhere on the surface of this planet, or just in this country?

Everywhere on the planet.

You must be very busy. Are there lots of others like you?

Yes.

Then I send greetings to all of your brethren, your fellow beings who do that, and I honour and support that process.

It's nice to be recognised.

I'm really glad you've come to share what you do with us. What can we best do as a result of meeting you?

Plant lots of flowers.

I'm not very good at that. Could you help me? Is that possible?

You could just go and spend time in the flowers.

Is there a name to refer to you and the others like you?

Nothing is apparent to me. When I ask is there a name, I get no.

We could use the term flower tickler!

I get a no to that.

Are you a kind of deva?

He is an elemental.

I could ask where you are on the agapé frequency scale. Would you know the answer to that?

It's okay to ask.

Would your agapé frequency be between 15 to 25,000?

No. 24,000 to 25,000.

You have responsibility for all species for flowering plants. That's in the range of elementals. So you're responsible for a wide range of plants. How do you manage?

By being happy everything's easy.

So your joy and love is something you find really easy to share with the flowers?

Yes.

Is that all that you do? Is that your whole purpose, whole activity?

No.

What other activities and responsibilities do you have? Might it be difficult to explain, or hard for us to understand?

Hard for you to understand.

I'm not surprised. Is this going to be our only opportunity to meet with you?

No.

In that case I invite Mica to bring you here again. Perhaps we can learn more about what you are and what you do. Or perhaps bring another representative of the kind of entity that you are, so we can learn more about you and the world that you live in. Is that possible?

Yes.

Then I would like to say thank you very much to Mica for taking this initiative. And thank you very much for being willing to join us and help us understand these things.

That's okay. It was good. Something different.

And an unexpected pleasure for you, I suspect.

[Laughs.] I like to have fun!

[Gone.]

◊ ◊ ◊

P [Channelling his guides.] *We intend to extend your understanding of that variety of identity. It is for this purpose that the assignation has been arranged between this group and the identity to whom you have chosen, for your convenience, to assign the name Mica.*

The purpose is multi-fold. We have the the opportunity to describe, in a comprehensive manner, those classes of identities that occupy the range of the agapéic scale from 15 to 25. It is a large population of identities, both in terms of species and in the number of identities per species. It is not possible to do more than sketch out the characteristics of a few of the species, but we intend to isolate and describe the characteristics of these species using modern terminology that unyokes them from the traditional descriptions of them that have accumulated over centuries. Those descriptions have magnified their characteristics, making them seem more complex than is actually the case due to an extensive overlay of human attributions.

On this occasion we wish to make you aware that the opportunity exists, and that various identities will be brought to you at mutually agreeable times. It is by our choice that this is happening. Naturally, we have the co-operation of the identities themselves, up and down the agapéic scale.

◊ ◊ ◊

[The following exchange took place a month later during a meditation session held on Trisha's family farm.]

T Guess who's here? *[Giggling.]* The flower tickler! He's chuckling to himself. I want to tickle Carolyn. He thinks that's really funny! *[Hilarious laughter.]* He's come to see you, Carolyn!

P I'm interested in learning from you. Tell us more about your role. Do you have days and nights, or are you always alert?

Days and nights. Flowers have to sleep, too.

When it's night in one place with one set of flowers what do you do? Do you go somewhere where it's light?

I curl up under the flowers.

Your hosts' family has an elfin figure on the bench out here. Is there anything about that that you recognise? Does it reflect your nature?

[Whispered response.] He's a bit slimmer than me.

Are you kind of round?

Round is good!

I think so, too. Do you sleep, or do you just rest?

I just close my eyes and rest. Sometimes I sing to the flowers.

Does that mean you have eyes?

Yes.

What do they see?

Flowers, more flowers.

Is that all you can see, all that's important?

They're the most important. But I can see grass, trees and other things.

We don't see people like you usually, because we have physical bodies and physical eyes that only see visible light. Do you see the same light as us, or something different?

Something different.

But you can see me right now, can't you?

No, we can see the person who's speaking for us. We don't see you.

There are some flowers on the table over there. Are you bigger or smaller than them?

Smaller.

How many of you are there?

There are many. There's one for each garden.

So like a community of flowers.

What about animals?

He's laughing again, a happy soul with no cares. He's not at all concerned about the animals. They don't bother him in the garden.

What about insects?

I don't give the insects much thought. They don't affect me.

So you love your flowers?

He feels like a flower child. I'm starting to wonder if he's on something. Pollen?

What does he do with a flower that's wilting or malformed? Or does he not bother with them and just attend to the healthy ones?

I try to fix them. I try to give them strength. But sometimes it's too late.

Some flowers only last for a day, don't they.

Yes.

I guess that means they serve their function in a day.

I encourage the new ones.

I got a picture of him tickling the buds. They're his beauties.

So this is a flower lover. A nurturer? Or a developmental overseer?

Nurturer. Helping them fulfil their potential, to be beautiful as they can.

What kind of beauty is best for flowers?

Strength.

So this is not a human conception of beauty?

Yes. They need to be strong and healthy.

C Are the gardens you work in the ones tended by humans, or are there other categories of garden you tend as well?

Anywhere there's flowers.

C So it could be a paddock?

Yes. Weeds are flowers, too. I asked about non-beneficial insects like greenfly. I got if the flowers are strong, vital and healthy those insects can't affect them.

That suggests that human appreciation is irrelevant. What about the impact of human activity on flowers, mass cultivation?

When I thought about big fields of tulips, or greenhouses with loads of flowers, I got a really queasy feeling.

Why?

It's not natural.

In what respect?

You're playing with nature.

Are those flowers able to fulfil their proper function?

No.

Is that a problem?

Yes.

So it's human exploitation that troubles you, rather than letting a plant go through its proper cycle, including old age and death.

Yes. Exploitation.

What do you do about it?

I can't help them, and that doesn't feel good.

When you say you can't help them, what do you mean by that?

They're closed off to me.

Envisaging a field of tulips, it's like they're faceless, characterless. There's nobody home. Like they've all had lobotomies.

C Well, they're cultivated.

They're weak.

P Because of genetic manipulation?

Yes.

Or because they've been selected for properties which relate to humans preferences, but not to their innate survival strengths?

Yes, they have no survival strengths.

It's very sad.

Does that mean you don't interact with them? Or don't like to?

I can't. They can't connect with me. They don't know how. I can out in the paddocks, and in gardens, where it's natural and they get the sun and the fresh air, the earth in their roots.

P Is this the case with hydroponically grown plants?

Oh, it's not good. Poor plants.

Do you communicate with the plants you care for and stimulate?

Just by me being there they get enveloped by my love, my energy. That's what they need.

Where do you get your energy supply from?

I have an endless supply!

Why?

Because I'm happy!

C You're a spark of universal light!

P Do you interact with any other orders of beings associated with plants? If your specialty is the flowers of plants, and all plants, what about the beings who foster particular kinds of plants? What's your relationship with them? Are you aware of each other? Do you interact?

We're aware of each other, but we do our own thing.

Can you give me examples of plants whose flower you attend to?

I'm getting yes to weeds, actual flowers, flowers on vegetables, on shrubs, but not flowers on trees.

P Why not trees?

Someone else looks after trees.

Is there another type of being who looks after other aspects of those plants?

Yes.

Do you interact at all? Are you aware of each other?

It's automatic. We each do our part.

Why doesn't the class of being associated with a particular plant deal with the flower of that plant?

Because it's my job!

Are there any flowering plants that you ignore apart from trees, that are beyond your responsibility?

No.

So trees are outside your responsibility. Why is that?

I'm too small.

Does that mean trees have big flowers?

C Trees have tree devas.

T Yes, I was getting big devas.

P It all seems very well organised. I'm curious about how old you are. You are aware of time?

Time doesn't matter at all.

Were you once younger than you are now?

I don't age. I just am. This just is.

Do you ever stop existing? Do you know that in the future there might be something else for you to develop and be able to do?

This is my job.

I'm very pleased you do this. Why have you come here today?

You were talking about flowers. I wanted to see the flower.

Did you see?

I did. [Giggles, looks at Carolyn. Earlier Peter had played a channelled communication comparing Carolyn's current life path to flowers.]

Tell me what she looks like to you?

If she was a flower she'd be a beautiful red rose.

Do you have anything to say to Carolyn, the flower?

Nurture yourself.

Why?

You deserve it. I will send you all my flower energy.

C Thank you.

P Is there anything else that you'd like to share with us?

You should all nurture the flowers.

Where are the flowers that you nurture? Are they close by?
This garden, but not the whole farm.

Does that mean Trisha can interact and connect with you? How will she know if she's looking at a flower you're nurturing?
She can talk to them, stroke them, offer them love and know I'm there.

Some humans sing to their gardens. What does that do?
Also offer them gratitude. Singing is good. Good energy.

I invite you to come back at any time you wish.
It's nice seeing you all.

Trisha seems to enjoy your energy very much! Can you recommend others that are in some way like you to come and talk with us, so that we can come to know them too?
I can't, but Mica can.

Are you here at his invitation?
He brought me the first time. It's time for me to go now.

Thank you very much for coming.
[Gone.]

T   And we still didn't get a name for him!

A New Year Eve's visit

The group's Christmas celebration involved sharing a meal, then meditating. It was followed by a surprising announcement regarding the theme for the coming year.

P [Channelling his guides.] *We have the opportunity on this occasion to convey a little more information about the organisation that brings individuals and groups to you, that you may share your love and assist them so they are accelerated on their journey. The organisation has depth. It is no exaggeration to claim that there are thousands of levels, each of which are monitored, sampled and surveyed in preparation for clearing.*

This is not surprising given living human beings occupy exactly those same thousands of levels, which you will understand from the models we have given you. Therefore it should also be understood that as there is a population per level, so there is also a residual resident population of those who have survived their deceased corpse, then continued in proximity to the physical, not knowing where to go or what to do. We have made plain the reasons this occurs over these past several years.

Of course, there are many more lost than have already been shared with you. It is by surveying and gathering from these different, multiple levels that we bring likely individuals to groups such as yours. Internationally, across this world and other worlds, many groups carry out this class of work. It has always been so. Yet there are fundamental misconceptions lying behind what have become traditional beliefs regarding this process.

In the distant past the human population existed in small hunter-gatherer groups. There were always one or two among them whose perceptions extended beyond the physical. They clamoured, or alternatively reluctantly began, to receive information about what lay beyond the senses. In the same way as here, those perceptive individuals were given the opportunity to interact with individuals who, after the death of their bodies, were uncertain, insecure, and lacked knowledge of their best options. After interacting with these lost, the perceptive individuals' easiest and most logical conclusion was, "Even though we don't know all these people we are sent, it must be that everyone who dies needs our intervention." That conclusion is an error.

We unambiguously assert that the appropriate number of those who are lost in darkness is around one percent. It is false to think that numerous individuals, constituting a high percentage of any population, need active intervention to save them from the fate of being lost after the death of their body, and so need to be retrieved, recovered, healed, counselled and, more conscious than before, dispatched to the light. This is a false assertion.

In part, the rise of this false idea can be associated with this time of the year, when, in [northern] cultures situated on the fringes of cold climates, movement was reduced and people had time for activities such as this. They found crowds of individuals who had not yet taken advantage of their opportunity to go on and eventually return. As a result, at the very beginnings of civilisation people were taught of the distinction between the personality and body, and the spirit outside them, at least as the distinction became manifest after death. This is how stories of the deceased came to accumulate through the centuries. And with them also developed the error.

Now we have the opportunity once again to thank you who are open to what exists beyond personality, beyond the physical, beyond the aura. You willingly come together in love to care for those who are fearful and, on occasion, to share the perceptions of those who are desperate to know that death is not their end. This all occurs in the context of your desire to train in mediumistic exploration. We give thanks for your willingness to meet, your continued attention, and your willingness to learn and to perform the tasks offered with loving goodwill. There is no greater love.

◊ ◊ ◊

T Mica's here. He has a message for us. I'm not sure how to put it into words, but it's something to do with seeing. My eyes are sore. I got a big strong yes feeling when I said that.

P Is this in relation to your own seeing?

T No, it's wider than that. It's the world.

People within the world?

Yes. They're not seeing.

Declining to see?

Yes.

From preoccupation?

From ignorance.

Of not knowing the necessity of looking in the right place?

Yes.

For what kind of information?

How to save the planet.

So, ecological concerns?

Yes.

Many people are concerned, but it's a minority.

I get a really really sad feeling from Mica.

How can we help? Do you have any suggestions?

He wants us to question all the elementals to educate people.

We met one that identified itself as a flower tickler. Are there others that can be regarded as knowledgeable authorities?

Yes.

It occurs to me that obtaining more information from representatives of the devic and elemental realms would give us the means to address these questions and share them with others. Is that feasible?

Yes. He felt kind of hopeful as you were saying all that.

Then I invite authoritative representatives from the community of the devic realm to speak to us, on the understanding that we will take responsibility for whatever material arrives and attempt to use it support the initiatives of eco-spiritualists and deep ecologists. Who is the best person to act as a channel for this information?

He says Carolyn.

She's busy tonight. Would it be best to send her an invitation on your behalf?

Yes. Another time.

What other ways may we be of assistance to you?

Keep doing what you're doing. Accept what you're hearing.

Thank you for the initiative. We'll attempt to convey your concerns to the appropriate communities.

Thank you for trying to help.

It's also our concern. Anything else?

He's hunkered down next to me. He's done, but he's still here.

Okay. Any other questions or comments?

I guess we just keep putting it out there and see who turns up.

It might need a developed strategy to do something effective with the material. We're accumulating it, but not doing much that's effective so far. I have a few people I've circulated some of this material to, but it's not systematic, and it's probably not to people who count, or who could be inspired by it and have the power to change anything.

Mmm.

I do feel there is actually a lot of potential to provide specific communications from a variety of different representative identities with direct responsibility for the natural world. And that could be combined with the theoretical models that we already have. But I feel quite some way away from achieving it. Perhaps that will have to be on the five year plan.

It needs to be from the group. I think it's best as a collaboration.

Keith Hill has already spoken of the possibility of a book based around the theme of people of the earth. This material could potentially be included. So if we could focus for several months, seeking communications from the devic level, then we could accumulate a bookful of material from which a suitable account could be crafted.

I got a yes for that from Mica.

Craig, is this something you have a specific interest in?

B Yep, always available.

T Mica said a big strong yes to you. He wants you.

B I know.

P I'm wondering if this is potentially a theme for part of the coming year, when we're not otherwise busy? I get the feeling that a clear, joint intention would facilitate the communication process. It appeals to me because I've had long-term concerns about the natural world and its balance, and how much humans beings are a scourge on the Earth. The green message needs all the support it can get.

B It's unanimous then. We'll be focussing on a different project.

R It would be good to review what we've got so far.

P Doing a little preliminary analysis may be helpful to start with, then we could look for where the gaps are. We could also look for supportive material to fill out their descriptions using the agapé scale. For example, we already have the flower tickler at 24-25. Having a way to structure the descriptions in a systematic way will add coherence. Without a structure we'll just end up with a bunch of stories, however interesting they are.

T Yes. Yes!

Categories of elementals

The following information was provided when Carolyn and Peter met outside the regular weekly meditation sessions.

C [Channelling.] *What needs to be identified is the nature of the different types of elementals, the abilities of each, and their capabilities for influencing the living. There are twelve main types, each with a different ability to influence the environment, and each with specific tasks for restoring balance and harmony where needed. The twelve main types are:*

12 Gatekeepers and watchers of those who enter special places, guarding them against gangs of marauding "baddies".

11 The sea. Oceans and fishes. Elementals called mermaids. They are generally unseen, but occasionally observed.

10 Mountains, alpine plant species.

9 Caves, grottos, crevasses and underground.

8 Savannah, dry open plains and deserts. Aboriginal people are familiar with these elementals.

7 Those airborne, floating in the atmosphere, using the air to survive.

6 Geology, rocks. I'm seeing rock strata and the little things that live on and around rocks, species like lichens, ferns and mosses.

5 Thermophilic species colonising undersea vents and in thermally active areas. I see steam and hot mud.

4 Grasses and forage species in grasslands.

3 Ferns, shaded places.

2 Flowers, sunny places.

1 Trees.

P This is very interesting because it fits with specifications outlined in *The Matapaua Conversations*, which referred to particular species being supported in specific environmental niches. You've just listed twelve environmental niches or habitats. Well done!

C [Surprised.] How about that!

P It's very interesting. But how are we to characterise elementals whose function is to give support to the range of species that occupy each of those environmental niches?

C [Channelling.] *The descriptions people have given of these beings resulted when they connected their third eye with their physical eye. What they perceive is then in a format that fits with the range of their knowledge and with caricatures present in their current personality. So they will adopt whatever image suits the perception of the moment. Obviously elementals are mobile spiritual energy forms. Anyone who may have seen them has speculated on their perception and personified them. Aborigines may have made them lizards or snakes because it fitted with what they knew. Chinese dragons were perhaps dust swept up by winds that were interpreted as living things, which later became mythical beings. What was seen really consisted just of bunched energy. In addition, all elementals have jobs to do. Knowing they are there doing their job, knowing they have messages to pass on to you, and protecting them is important. Recognising their existence, and being open to receiving messages from them to act on to avoid calamities, is useful.*

Is any credence at all to be given to traditional imagery associated with this class of being?

Yes. It is a way of distinguishing something that exists. If you put an image and name to it, it doesn't matter what the image or name is because they help characterise their existence. You can call it what you like. The element of magic and mystery describes what people know it as.

So it's a tool for recognising the existence and variety of different species?

Yes. There's also the likes of leprechauns that I'm now asking about. Evidently there are disembodied spirits that mischievously play around by simulating elementals. They're a separate class, so you can get them mixed up.

Are you saying that is a different class of elemental than the ones whose function it is to care for the life forms?

Yes. The mischievous, disembodied ones pretend they are carers. There are the carers of the forest, and there are the mischievous ones who pretend to be them.

Why?

Because it's fun. The mischievous ones do it. Mica's a real one.

I think we will need a lot more discussion on these points.

◊ ◊ ◊

The following was communicated to Peter nine weeks later.

P [Channelling his guides.] *We come on this occasion to continue the delivery on the important distinctions between elementals and other aspects of the model of agapéic space, as well as to offer more information about the elementals themselves, as distinct from devas of various other kinds.*

There are some terminology difficulties and confusions which first need to be clarified. The term elemental includes the devas of other species. The elemental, which exists in the range 15 to 25 on the agapéic scale of agapéic frequency, is a kind of supervisor which is focussed explicitly on an environmental niche rather than on any individual species living within the niche. That is the first distinction.

The second distinction is that the elementals responsible for different environmental niches are not different from one another, merely focussed in a different direction for similar purpose.

Third, the elementals which may validly be called devas are those that are focused on the support of individual life species. The distinction between devas is one of kind, not of class, in the sense that lovingly attending to and caring for life is the same in all devas.

In fact, elementals are not fundamentally distinct from the nodes of Dao-consciousness, as we are calling them, relating to the human species, for humans are on one level simply another animal. The distinction is, as we have explained at length elsewhere, that the individual node of Dao-consciousness is focussed on one individual rather than a group or class of individuals. Having clarified these matters at least that far, we will continue.

The desire you show to introduce these matters into the public arena is exemplary. It is a large task. We hope we are not confusing you too much by introducing descriptions which are somewhat at odds with traditional descriptions, but traditional descriptions have become confused due to the variety of motifs from different cultures being carried forward through time.

Related to this confusion is the term and attributes of soul. Soul is a highly contaminated term and is best dispensed with in this context, as we have done. What we are offering is intended to be a significant reintroduction of clarified concepts via a modern set of descriptions and models. You have asked for a comprehensive listing of the elementals and their activities. We will provide this.

The first class already encountered experientially is that of the undine, to use that term, the elemental focussed on water. Within water are numerous environmental niches, given water is distributed across the planet. Elementals in the form of devas directly associate with each individual species occupying niches in water. Therefore it is appropriate that the undine has a supervisory role, because it comprises the class that oversees the over-arching watery environment.

In the same way, other elementals are associated with the environment of air. Living within this environment are those species that partly or largely occupy the gaseous atmosphere. That also covers a very wide variety of species, insects and flying animals in particular. We won't name the set of the associated elementals at this time, for it incorporates too broad a class.

As previously encountered, there is a group of elementals associated with and responsible for the earthly environment. That is, the thin layer of soil, as it is commonly termed, which many species inhabit for the purposes of living and procreating.

Those are the three prime environments. Within each are many sub-environments. There are corresponding sub-identifications yet to be made of the appropriate elementals responsible for each. It is not our intention at this time to provide a complete listing, merely to indicate the general classification which can be used, these being, earth, water and sky.

Two elementals and a traveller

T I have an elemental. Not Mica.

R Welcome. Who are you?

I'm standing guard.

What are you standing guard over?

Flowers.

All sorts of flowers, or one particular type?

All of them.

Where is your domain? Where are the flowers you're guarding?

It's the whole of New Zealand. A level above the flower tickler. The high heid yin [supervisor] for the flowers.

Does that include trees and small plants?

No, just flowers.

What are you guarding against?

I'm overseeing the other elementals.

Is there a hierarchy of elementals?

There's one more level between me and the flower tickler.

How may we be of service to you?

We're just pleased to know you're aware of us.

I'm pleased to be aware of you, too. Is there something we should know about caring for flowers?

Show them love.

Is there anything in particular you'd like to say to other humans?

Be more aware.

Thank you. Does anyone else have questions or comments?

C I'm thinking of the flowers grown commercially, in glass houses. I wonder if they're happy being forced to grow all times of the year?

They're not happy. I can't do much for them but let them know I'm here.

I guess they're grown to make people happy. It's nice to know that they're treasured.

It's not ideal.

R What *is* ideal?

Grow them yourself. Nurture them and appreciate what goes into producing them.

K Do the flowers accept that when they are starting to wither we prune them back to let new growth come? Is that unacceptable?

It's acceptable.

It doesn't sadden the flower?

No.

It saddens me sometimes.

They're already gone at that stage. It keeps them healthy.

R If we acknowledge the elementals that are caring for plants, flowers, and other aspects as well, does that benefit elementals?

Yes.

K Humans probably had a better relationship with elementals many years ago. Would that be correct?

Yes.

R Do you have a name, something that we can call you?

You can call me the Guardian.

[Gone.]

◊ ◊ ◊

T I have someone watching us. Not a higher being. He happened on us by chance. We seem to get a lot of these, don't we?

R Welcome. How can we be of service to you?

Who are you?

Just a group of friends who get together and meditate, and communicate with beings like yourself.

Hmm. That's different.

Who are you, may we ask?

I'm a traveller.

Have you been in human form?

No.

How would you describe yourself, apart from as a traveller?

Energy.

Do you have a home?

I don't need a home.

So you're not from a particular place? You simply travel?

That's right.

What's your purpose in travelling?

To expand.

Your energy, consciousness?

Awareness.

K For yourself? Or for others?

Myself.

R How may we help you or be of service to you?

I'm just observing.

Do you find us interesting?

Yes. I don't have many conversations with humans.

I guess not many humans are able to converse in this way.

No.

Are there many travellers like yourself?

Very many.

Where do you travel?

Anywhere and everywhere. It's very enjoyable.

Do you travel into the physical dimension that we're in?

No. I don't want to be trapped. But I can look from the outside.

K Do you have any advice for us?

Be kind.

R We welcome your presence, and appreciate that you made yourself known and told us a little bit about yourself.

[Gone.]

T He had a nice feeling. Serene.

[No one had a visual impression.]

◊ ◊ ◊

T I have a sad elemental. My head is hanging.

P Hello and welcome. Why are you sad?

There's no hope.

For?

The Earth.

Why do you feel like that?

Chemicals are poisoning it.

Which chemicals?

The chemicals farmers use.

What are they using those chemicals for?

Weed killers.

Why are weed killers used on a farm a problem?

It accumulates.

Where?

In the soil.

Why is that a problem?

It kills the microbes.

The soil bacteria?

Yes. Then there's no life left in the soil.

What happens to the other soil animals? They die too?

Yes.

Where is this happening?

Everywhere.

C What about big farms where they grow cotton for thousands of acres. Are they using pesticides to grow huge crops?

Mostly.

P Is that the kind of situation you're referring to?

One of them. It's just one example.

C Food crops as well?

Yes.

Is there anything we can do?

You need to change your thinking. You need to feed the soil.

Will it stop feeding us if we don't look after it?

It can do it, but it won't be good for you. You're not getting any nutrients from that kind of food.

P I understand your feelings. I'm wondering, have you come to us of your own accord, or is this a message delegated to you as a task?

It's personal. I knew you would listen.

Where are you normally located?

The whole world.

Does that mean we're speaking to you as a representative of the collective opinion of the world of the deva?

Yes.

Are you responsible for many many others?

Yes. I don't know what to tell them. We're fighting a losing battle.

Then you understand the commercial forces that push humanity do these things. Is that correct?

Yes. They're the problem.

Do you see the effective communication of your message as being on the Earth-loving political level? Or on another level?

To people who understand the Earth.

I understand that in a sense it's not your problem. You're simply passing a well informed opinion. Is that correct?

Yes. But it makes me sad.

I expect it does. You have that weight of responsibility, and simultaneously a sense of powerlessness, and most of humanity doesn't admit your existence, let alone your feelings. Can you see the future?

I despair for the future.

Do you know that many humans also have such feelings?

Yes. It's too big a change.

So humanity is destroying the fertility on which it depends?

Yes.

My personal understanding of these things is that the solution is a radical reduction of population. What's your opinion on that?

That's not the solution.

I'm interested to know that.

Each person needs to take responsibility and change what they're doing.

C Is that related to consumerism?

Yes. Think about what you're buying, where it came from. And grow your own food.

Using traditional or biological farming methods?

Or organic.

P What's your opinion of groups such as this conveying your feelings and enabling you to be listened to?

If you just make a change yourself and spread the word, impress the need on other people, encourage them to make a change, it should snowball.

Is there anything else in your opinion that would be worth doing in order to enable others to know of these things?

Stay aware and keep remembering the earth and keep remembering us.

Is there any other particular way that we can help you?

Listening was enough.

I certainly value your willingness to communicate in this way. I acknowledge the rare presence you comprise, and value that.

Nothing more. He's gone. When he said "listening was enough" I felt like a weight lifted off my shoulders. When you flattered him, thanking him for coming, and he went all shy, like he was blushing.

It's a very big claim, to be a world elemental. Do you think that was accurate?

World elemental for the soil. I had this feeling like a caring boss would feel about his workers, "Oh, I don't know what to say to them." Like he could see what the true situation is, but they're all just going about their business and don't see the bigger picture.

So, a genuine supervisory role. Top level for this planet.

At the beginning he was so sad. About two thirds through it changed to resignation.

Rescues, a rejection and moving on

T Someone is with me, but I don't know who or what. The feeling is of being perplexed.

P Welcome to our circle. How may we reduce your confusion?

T They aren't here for the circle. It's something to do with me. It's Timothy! What had been going through my mind was, "I'm open to anything. I'm happy to help. Help me know when the right horse appears for me, and please let me have some joy again." [Trisha was grieving the recent death of her horse, Tay.] It's like he's saying, *What's this thing about joy, why do you need joy?* He still doesn't get it.

C *You people are very odd.*

P It's the nature of being human. What's your nature?

Not human.

Is there a word or phrase that would describe identities like you?

I just am.

Are any of our emotions or mental attributes familiar to you?

Peacefulness. I don't understand these spikes of emotion.

For some of us peacefulness is a rare condition and so is sought. Is peacefulness a normal condition for you?

Yes.

Is that why you're here to examine us?

To examine her.

Explain your particular interest in Trisha.

What she's going through right now is interesting.

Can you be more specific?

Those spikes of emotion.

Interesting? Or educational?

Perplexing. I don't quite understand it.

How can we help you understand?

Why can't you humans just be more accepting?

It's an attachment, and grieving a loss.

But there is no loss.

Please explain.

She may have lost her friend, this horse, in this life. But nothing ends. She's still there.

Where's "there"?

The energy is still around.

Close by?

Yes.

In what kind of space?

The analogy I'm getting is it's like you and I were friends and you got on a train and went away somewhere. We're not together any more, but you're still there.

So distance, but not true absence. Please explain your concept of the destination of this friend, Tay.

She's just somewhere else doing something else. Your concept of death limits you. Just accept it. I don't understand why you get so upset about it.

It may have to do with human reward systems. Emotional contact is reinforced by tactile information, which causes pleasure. The absence of that stimulus affects us emotionally. Is that within your experience?

I understand what you're saying, but it's not necessary.

True. But humans become attached to those experiences.

Interesting. You don't need that attachment to show love. You can show love in other ways. You're limiting yourself.

Can you cite some other ways?

This person, by saying that the relationship has ended in death, she's causing herself grief. Just accept that the relationship has changed, not ended. There's no need to feel these spikes of emotion.

I'm interested that you use the term "spike". What do you mean?

It seems there's deep grief, then now she's looking for joy. Why can't you just be on an even keel? There really isn't anything to be upset about.

It's in the nature of the human. We form attachments for survival and procreation.

Seems like a hard way to live to me.

We sometimes find it so!

Thank you for your clarifications. I will just observe the rest of your meeting, if that's okay.

You're most welcome to do so. We value contact with you and look forward to encountering you again.

[As Trisha drove home from the meditation session later that night, she saw Tay galloping beside the car.]

◊ ◊ ◊

C A word has sprung into my mind. Posh. I don't have any other words or particular feelings. I feel very calm. I'm inspecting everyone. I'm resigned to my condition.

P I invite you to actively engage with the opportunity we offer to you, out of love and goodwill and willingness to be of service. You seem to have some beliefs about your prospects. What are they?

This is it.

This is not it. You are mistaken.

Well, it's been this for a while.

It doesn't matter how long, this isn't the end. What has your culture taught you about what happens after death?

Nothing.

I'm sure it did. You may not have paid attention, but the messages will be within you. What are they?

I guess I thought I was in some sort of limbo and I just have to wait it out.

Precisely.

So I'm waiting. I'm just here. It's okay. I don't mind.

Do you understand that this is not your first death?

No.

You would in all probability have passed this way at least one hundred times before. Why don't you remember?

Well, exactly! If I had I would.

Look deeper. Lift your horizons. Open yourself to external input. What do you see? If you look upwards, downwards, all around.

I see a thin line of light over on the horizon.

What do you suppose that might represent?

Don't know, but I don't think it was there before.

This already constitutes progress and change from where you have been. That is your destination. What do you expect to find there?

I have no idea!

Who loved you, and for all you know loves you still?

That's an upsetting question.

Then share it with us. It's a question worth asking.

My husband loved me.

Is he alive or dead?

Dead.

Then call out to him.

I don't think he'll want to see me now.

You might be surprised. As an insurance policy, who else loved you? Did you have a mother?

Yes.

Did she love you?

That was never clear.

Is she alive or dead?

Dead.

Then call out for her as well.

I'd rather call my aunt.

Is she alive or dead?

Alive.

Then she's not as available. Who else? A father?

He was never there.

That might be irrelevant.

My mother was fairly indifferent to me. I guess I could call on my father.

Try it. See what happens. As part of the process, image yourself moving faster and faster towards that light. There are more people looking for you than you imagine, who love you. Can you see them?

Yes.

Go to them. They will welcome you. Start the next phase of your journey.

[Gone.]

C I saw what I think was her father in the forefront, but unformed. But there were three girls, cousins, waving, encouraging her to come. They put their arms around her and lead her off.

◊ ◊ ◊

T Now I feel shifty. My eyes are looking around. I'm looking for an angle or something.

P What's your deepest fear?

T *I don't feel scared.*

What's the worst that could happen?

This is a visitor, not a spirit needing to be rescued. Not Timothy.

Please tell us about yourself. How can we contribute to your experience?

I don't want anything from you.

Then why are you here?

I'm not sure I want to say. It's none of your business.

One of the rules of this particular place is honesty.

Interesting.

Another rule is loving regard. That means goodwill. Are you comfortable with those things?

I don't really see the necessity. [Trisha felt her lip curling, like a sneer.]

How old are you?

You've got a lot of questions, don't you?!

I do. Are you human, or were you? If you're human, do you know you're dead? How did you arrive here?

He's trying to decide whether to say anything!

Did you fall? Or were you pushed?

Nobody pushes me!

I suspect they had to to get you here, because by the looks of you you didn't come by choice.

You can think what you like.

T He's not human. When you said, "If you are human, do you know you're dead?" the thought was there's no such thing as death. He was just passing by.

P Thank you for your reluctant introduction. We are very pleased usually to meet all individuals, whatever their nature and status.

I have no interest in you people.

Then our blessings be with you, wherever you choose to be.

You can keep your blessings! Strange people.

T He's moving on now.

P He was obviously looking for something, and we weren't it.

◊ ◊ ◊

T I'm feeling queasy again.

R How can we be service to you?

T *Wait a minute, where did you come from?*

We're just sitting here, and are available to you for talking and help should you wish it.

Do I need help?

I don't know, do you?

I was doing okay.

Then you're happy where you are? What can you see around you?

I suppose it's quite nice to have company.

When did you last have company?

Long time. Can't remember.

What was the year when you died?

1735.

You have been waiting around on your own for a long time! What did you do when you were embodied?

Can't remember. It's too long ago.

Did you have family, people around you?

No.

Do you remember loved ones?

Vaguely.

Remember a wife, parents, sisters or brothers?
I had a sister.
Would you like to have the company of your sister again?
Sure.
Look around and call out for your sister. She will likely appear.
Just like that? I think I can see her.
Take yourself over there.
Gone. Her name was Isabel. I didn't get his.

◊ ◊ ◊

T My head has been turned to the right.
P Welcome. What have you to share with us?
I'm just looking.
Why?
You seem different.
In what way? Using what for comparison?
I was just drawn to you.
Please share something about yourself. What is your nature?
I'm a level above you.
What does that mean?
I'm not human any more.
So you were?
Yes.
Did you live more than once?
Yes.
How many times did you live?
Four hundred and fifty-seven.
Why is it that you are no longer human?
I moved on.
To what? Is that something you can answer? Is it permitted?
It is permitted.
You mean you anticipate never coming back into a human body?
Yes, correct.
What about any other kind of body, any other kind of species?

Yes, perhaps.

Does that imply it would occur somewhere other than this planet?

Yes.

Within this particular galaxy?

No.

What options are you aware of?

I'm not sure. But I'm in a peaceful place and open to anything.

Do you have any idea about the number of options that you have, or is that not in your awareness yet?

I'm not yet aware.

When you say you're at the next level, in what terms? Is it on the level of agapéic frequency, hierarchy or willingness to bequest agapé?

Hierarchy.

What difference do you observe in that change?

I no longer worry. It's very peaceful.

Is that something any human can expect to make, that kind of transition?

Yes.

Is it something that happens automatically?

It's not automatic.

Is there a particular criterion or set of criteria that apply?

He's gone. It was like someone pressed the off switch. My head went down and he was gone. It felt like he was hovering just above us, looking down, and that he didn't come across people like us very often.

P I don't recall another identity like that from just one level up, who claims he no longer needs to incarnate as a human. If that's the case, it means he's dealt with all his karma, which I'd have thought was unusual. A data outlier. He did have a reasonably strong presence.

◊ ◊ ◊

T Now it feels like there's someone way up to the right.

P [Channelling his guides.] *We come among you to affirm the level of identity and self-description of the previous visitor. It is, as you have concluded,* an unusual individual who deviates from the norms we have proposed in our models. The implication that it was not bound for further incarnation is not correct. The implication that it is bound for embodiment in other species is correct. It forms one of the smaller subsets of the population bound for species crossover.

Only an individual of unusual competence and creativity seeks to master a second species and learn to control a second body type. It is with particular interest that we introduce this, specifically for the purpose of indicating the further reaches of the spectrum of experience available to individuals seeking experience through embodiment. We have come tonight because the group is less troubled by anxious identities seeking release, which presents an opportunity to discuss the spectrum of models given to date. We therefore invite questions from you to clarify any confusions.

What percentage of spirits is able to cross species like that?

The opportunity is available to all, but only a small percentage take it, around three percent. The task of mastering one body type is normally sufficient. Relinquishing, resolving and responding to karma occupies most of each individual's lives. Only the unusually competent empower themselves in this way.

How is it decided what their next species would be?

They are made aware of options, but they choose.

How does it affect their total number of incarnations?

It may affect it or it may not. Typically it does, of course, because even for a competent individual a second species may easily take a similar period of time to master as it took to master the first. Although commonly there are efficiencies gained in the process, which means that obtaining competence in the second species likely requires a smaller number of incarnations. Naturally, there is some similarity between embodied species, but the differences can be extreme, depending on how the characteristics of the second species compare to those of the first. Embodied species constitute a wide diversity of populations. Obviously, some cluster into similar aspects, and others do not. So if one initially chose one species that is different from most others, and then a second species which is also different from most others, it means a great disparity of operating techniques, if one could phrase it that way, are required to be learnt.

Of course, if one chose a second species out of a group which was similar in nature to the first, then the learning curves would be closer and facility gained much faster.

Is two the maximum number of species a spirit would incarnate into?

No, it is not, but three is extremely rare. Usually two is more than sufficient to satisfy what every individual needs, which is to make the necessary shifts in their nature so they are no longer required to return to a state of physical embodiment. This principle does not vary across species. All species are subject to the same protocols, in the sense of engaging with learning, and working through the consequences of learning, the consequences of making mistakes, resolving mistakes, and continuing to learn, until obtaining mastery of the particular species in question. Often that is quite sufficient to reinforce the character traits that facilitate their transition out of the need to reincarnate.

Thank you for sharing that information.

We are delighted to find the level of confusion is so low that it required only a very brief set of responses. We leave you now.

P That was nice. It's been a while since we've had a visitation from that level. I'm interested that you had the clear perception of it being a long way away.

T It was way, way up, on the right.

P Steeply up and on the right.

T Yes. The previous guy was literally just here. I knew he was just a level above us. He had a very peaceful feeling.

P Interesting that would come with just one step up in the hierarchy. But he might be quite far from the norm.

A rock elemental and advice

Some time before Trisha had bought a piece of pounamu (greenstone, jade) while visiting Waiheke Island. The pounamu occasionally manifested a need to be held, which Trisha did. Earlier in the day she felt it wanted to come to that evening's meditation session, so she brought it.

T Just now I said to myself, would the spirit associated with this piece of pounamu like to come forward and make themselves known to us. I got a worried feeling.

P You're most welcome to join us.

T I feel like I'm hiding, curling up, pulling inside myself. I get no for a he or a she, and yes for elemental.

P I invite you to feel welcome, safe, and possibly understood. Please share the reason for your desire to curl up and hide, because you don't need to do that here.

T He's an elemental for rocks. He says they're stripping the land.

P Stripping the land? Where?

When they dig things up. Taking these [the pounamu] *out of the land. They should leave them where they are.*

Is this any particular kind of rock?

All rock.

Really? Humans shift a lot of rock. We dig it up, crush it, make roads, move it all over the place. Why is that a problem?

How can I look after the rocks if you keep breaking them up?

That's a very good question. When you say look after, what is it about rock that concerns you or requires your attention? Is it the rocks themselves? Or the communities of life on the rocks?

The rocks themselves.

You've been attached to a particular piece of rock that could have come from the South Island of this country. It's called greenstone. Is that special to you?

All rock is special.

Have you only lived in the islands of this country, New Zealand?

No.

Where else have you lived?

India.

If you can travel from India to this country, is that easy for you?

No.

If it's not easy why did you change location?

New Zealand needed protection.

So when did you come here?

I came here when things started to change.

Did they start to change when humans came?

Before that.

Was it change by volcanic action?

When the first humans arrived here. Those humans used stone in their lives, in very active ways.

What do you protect about rocks?

Their majesty. They should be revered and left complete.

Do you protect mountains?

Yes, from mountains down.

How does it affect you when humans take a rock and change it?

It changes everything.

Taking one rock out of a river bed changes the river. Why is that a bad thing?

T That's perplexed him a bit. On the one hand I'm seeing the course of rivers being changed, on the other he's going, hmmm, I sort of see your point. *It's not always a bad thing. But there's a snowball effect.*

P So have you been hurt or damaged in any way by these actions of humans? How has it changed your existence?

We're constantly uprooted.

Do you develop attachment to the location where you are in association with a particular set of rocks?

Sort of. But it's bigger than that.

I'm thinking that the landscape of rock must be, if the natural rate of change of weathering, etc.

How can I keep track of them if they're always moving?

Exactly. I was just thinking that the natural landscape is so stable for such long periods of time, that any accelerated rate of change would be a problem.

We would prefer there were no humans.

I expect you would. It would simplify your existence. So is your task to know where each rock is?

I have to know where they are if I'm going to protect them.

The piece Trisha brought tonight is clearly part of a much larger rock. It must have been cut into many pieces which could be all over the world. Do you need to know where every bit of each rock is now?

It makes me very sad. I lose track of a lot of them.

Is that like a failure of duty?

I suppose.

R You said before, *we* would prefer. Are there more than one of you, elementals for rocks?

There's more than just me.

Do you experience powerlessness in this loss?

Yes.

That's very depressing. Humans experience that. There must have been a big increase in powerlessness as humans have multiplied across the world, for people like you?

Yes.

That's sad. Most humans have no understanding at all of this. Is that your experience?

Yes. It would help if people spoke to us, told us what they were doing, warn us, and not just do it.

The response most humans would make to what you've just said is complete disbelief. Most only see others like themselves. They don't see people like you, so the understanding that you even exist isn't present in their minds. How can we help?

They need to respect the land.

What do you mean by respect?

Tread carefully. Be grateful. Don't just pillage it.

Would it help if more people understood there is a community of beings in every part of the land, beings such as yourself and other identities helping and protecting all species?

Yes! Can you do that?

We can try. Some know of and value that kind of understanding. They feel, and some can talk with, identities such as yourself, and deva. I think all we can do is reinforce the idea that a landscape contains many beings, most of which are not visible to human eyes.

Yes. Whatever you can do is appreciated.

I commit to making the record of our conversation with you available to the world via our website. Thank you for your presence here with us, share your feelings with us.

Thank you for listening.

You're most welcome.

[Gone.]

P How does that leave you feeling?

T Sad. But I could feel his hopes getting up when you said we could find a way to communicate with people and pass on what he said. Do elementals incarnate over and over like humans?

P They live and die. But we're just scratching the surface with the information we have.

◊ ◊ ◊

P My attention is now being drawn over to the left hand side. I'm getting some impressions of something like a six-legged insect. I don't quite know what this is.

C I heard "observer". Just watching.

T I'm getting that, too. And right before you spoke I had a flash of white light for a few seconds.

P I'm curious about this observer. I'd like to dialogue if I could.

C *The interpretation you've made of the observation being of insect life is just an interpretation. We're not a species at all. It's a visual interpretation you've made of our form. We aren't a species as such.*

P You don't associate with a physical form?

No.

R What's your role?

Research. Watching. Interpreting.

P Specifically humans?

No. Interactions between humans and devas and what you call other energies. We're sitting by, just observing.

P Then welcome.

If it's alright, we'll be present for a while.

Certainly.

R What do you find interesting about humans like us?

The current communication, conversation. The nature of your ability to communicate and assist those disembodied souls who pass you by.

P What are your observations of them. Are they truly in need?

Nobody comes to you who isn't in need of some sort. Your participation in this method of soul assistance is of interest to us. It is specialised.

According to your observations, how do these souls arrive into our proximity?

Your openness to allow them.

Many say that they don't know how they have arrived here; we assume the agency is other identities in spirit. Is that your observation?

C It seems like we form a gateway, a visibility that allows them to be drawn to us.

Guidance from other sources is quite possible, allowing them to open their eyes to see your gateway. There are those like us who observe and are aware of this opportunity for any who are indeed lost. We are impressed, very impressed. Hence our visit to you this evening.

P I always presumed we are one of many assemblies of people who perform this function. Is that your observation?

It depends what you think many is. It's very specialised and opportune.

I presume that we are one of at least many thousands distributed across the face of this planet.

At times there may be in the thousands, yes. Groups come and go.

R   You mentioned communication with devas. Have you any comments on that?

It's our observation that it has taken place before. We are interested in watching reciprocal communication between such forms, and the advice and information that you can assimilate, share and publicise. Make people more aware of how the energies work. We're interested in observing if that should occur again.

What will you do with your observations?

Share with a network of identities who help those who are lost.

P   In relation to the deva communications, what advice do you have in terms of what exactly we should do with those observations? Using the term "deva communications" covers of all sorts of different energies.

The word deva is just a label, a name for the various intelligences you come across. You've met many so far, and are aware there are many more. You have an ability that enables different energies to come and educate you. Your interest in learning from them is applauded. It leads to greater understanding, which can only be for the good.

Do you perceive that to be our role?

A strong role.

Is it also a responsibility?

Yes.

What would happen if we declared ourselves unwilling?

All forms of openness would close. All avenues would close. They wouldn't come.

Were we to say nothing, you say that communication would cease. Were we to say, yes, we'll make the information available, but only after the death of all in the group, would that constitute any impediment or barrier to the ongoing communication?

That would indicate a fear, and you wouldn't be doing this if you had such fear. So by being open to communication, as you're doing with us at the

moment, indicates you have little fear of communicating or of the implica-
tions of communicating with us.

That's perfectly accurate, of course.

If you had fear, you wouldn't be doing this. Our belief is that you will
potentially do this for many years. We feel like you have the strength, abil-
ity and power to interpret conversations from all sorts of energies and record
them for the potential education of many people for many years, for decades,
to come. The work you do is already well known. We are only here because we
know you don't fear us.

By saying that, do you thereby identify yourselves as a member of
the devic clan or category?

We aren't a member of a category as such, no.

Is there any observation you could make as to improving those
capacities? Or is what we're doing to date adequate?

You're more than adequate in your commitment and dedication.

Presuming the information was uploaded to at least one website,
is that sufficient as a means of promulgating these encounters?

At this time, that is sufficient.

Thank you for that confirmation.

For those who need to hear this information, it's sufficient. Technology
and receptivity will change in due course. What you have at the moment is
highly adequate.

Thanks for your attention.

Thank you for your commitment. It doesn't go unnoticed. In fact, it is
celebrated.

In relation to our intention of walking up a hill in a couple of
weeks, do you have any recommendations for that day?

You will be guided by those who have invited you there.

Thank you.

Meeting a deva on Maungatautari

Carolyn and Peter had previously been invited by elementals to visit Maungatautari, a protected ecological sanctuary surrounded by a pest-proof fence. Established in 1912, the sanctuary provides a home for some of Aotearoa's many endangered plants, birds and lizards.

P *[Speaking into a recorder]* We're here on Maungatautari mountain with the afternoon sun piercing the clouds, resting at a flat point in the steep track alongside one of the fences. On the way in the car Carolyn got a message stating that the invitation was for her and I to be present, which is why the others are not here. It's for an expanded introduction to the hierarchy among life forms here, including, presumably, the devic population. I don't remember what else was said.

C Have fun. I think that's what they said. Have a nice afternoon.

P Alright. It was 3pm when we arrived at the end of the road. I don't know how far this easy-walking road goes, or where it turns into a proper bush track. And I don't know how far we need to go. But I guess we'll just stop and rest and consult the devas to find out. Carolyn stopped further up the road, saying her head was hurting.

P Your face is all scrunched up.

C Mm.

P Why is your head sore?

C I don't know. Ow! We're entering a special place.

P Special to whom?

C Those that invited us.

P [Walking on.] I'm feeling a distinct pressure in my chest. It feels to be on the hara level in the chest. It's gone again now. ... We've come to a fork in the track and a sign that says, OVER THE MOUNTAIN: THIS

WAY PLEASE. The very easy road continues further up. This alternative track we're on is wet and slushy and goes through overhanging bush. It's dark, wet and tortuous. Carolyn's just disappeared on up there so perhaps I should follow her. I get: *We would prefer that you do so.* Okay. ... Why did you turn up this track instead of the easy way?

C Because this is where we had to go.

P How did you know that?

C 'Cause it is.

P So just a knowing? Okay. [*Both puffing with exertion now.*] To my astonishment I just said silently, "I bow before those who invited us." This in the context of saying at other times, "I bow to no man!" ... [*Aloud.*] It might pay to be alert to signs.

C I'm looking for a sign to put my plastic bag down and sit on it. It might be not too far away.

P [*Finding a seat-like root making a step on the path.*] Here?

C Yep.

P 15:59. [*Sitting down on the track.*]

C 4 o'clock! 2 o'clock deciding to go, 3 o'clock get here, 4 o'clock we found it.

P So it's an hour's walk back to the car.

C It'll get dark.

P Yes, but not till six. ... I give greetings to the identities present on this Maungatautari mountain. Having only a slight understanding of the dynamics and relationships between such identities, for my own benefit, and the benefit of others, I wish to learn more of who lives here and why, their lifestyle and life purpose, their principal activities, functions and proclivities, and their destination at death. I give thanks to my good friend Carolyn for independently confirming that today was the day. I note the relatively high level of bird life and seek a description, if available, of the impact on the inhabitants of this mountain of that pest-free enclosure, and what meaning that has had to those who live here, rather than just for the humans who dreamed it, planned it, built it and maintain it. What is best for the lifetime for this mountain and its protection? ... I get somebody saying, *You ask many questions!* Yes, I do. I'm very grateful for the opportunity to understand much more about such things. ... I'm seeing someone just manifest, rather tall, just over to the right of us. I had the impression that we were to come with him and that we can safely leave our bodies here. Okay, let's go.

[Peter: Carolyn did. But as far as my ordinary awareness informed me, I did not. But I did sit on a thick jersey to insulate my gluteus maximi from the cold earth.]

P Would it be correct to presume that in Maori mythology, the patupaiarehe—the people of the mist, I think is the meaning of that phrase—are in fact the spiritual occupants of places such as this, as recorded during human occupation prior to Europeans? I seem to get a qualified yes to that. What do you get?

C Mm-mm.

P [Channelling.] *Spiritual inhabitants, who live far beyond the lifetime of humans, have been resident here for countless millennia, ever since the land rose from the sea. As this small island group was suitable for populating, it was populated by a variety of targeted species, including migratory species and unique species. A young country, it didn't need controlling predatory species, as the conventional inter-species competition for food was sufficient.* ... How are you getting on, Carolyn?

C I'm just getting cold.

P So is this just an initial foray to familiarise ourselves with the requirements of being here?

C [Channelling.] *Those who look after the mountain are entities who choose to protect the trees, ground and atmosphere, and nurture generations on generations of all the plant species and plant life on the mountain. So we are like other entities who look after the flowers. We're just the ones who look after the mountain and ecosystems like these in the higher regions of different countries. There are also those who live on the ground, on the very top of the ground and underground just on the surface. These look after the earth so the seeds that fall will grow and regenerate. Then there are those who live in the trees.* I'm seeing something like fairies that flit around like birds, and with the birds in the trees. *They're a special type that offers a particular*

*level of nurturing care for the birds and their nests and just under the tree's top
canopy. The one you met previously was the Guardian. He's the one who lives
up here and watches all the others. Documented in various forms of Irish and
Scandinavian mythology, and others, are those that look after forests. They
are depicted in a variety of ways. The vision you had is just one of the ways
that we can be seen.*

P The lingering impression I have is of a tall slim log of wood that
is aware, alert and commanding.

C You visited his patch. He invited you and is interested in sharing knowledge about the ecosystem up here. [Channelling.] *You are
very welcome to enjoy it and appreciate it. Others who walk through the bush
and forest just trample it on their way somewhere else. They admire it to a certain extent, but don't understand the intricacies and the spiritual level of those
who are also here in the forest. So it was nice to meet you when you came before,
and nice to have you back. ...* There seem to be the ground-level carers,
the fairy type that flies around with the birds and looks after the birds
in the nests, and then the Guardian who keeps watch over everybody.

P So is he the top of the local hierarchy?

C Yes.

P Is there a particular sequence in hierarchy?

C No. He just watches over the other entities.

P So is this simply a geological feature that offers such individuals a convenient territory for which to care?

C The geological feature this high is protected by its own guardian. The bush has its own types of minders, just as the valleys and the
grasses in the gardens have their types. This is the bush type. A larger
alpine area would still have a guardian of the mountain. Then there
are those who look after the creatures in the rocks or bush. They're
different energies looking after nature in the bush.

P And is the hierarchy based on an authoritarian stance?

C No.

P Or loving nature and capacity to be responsible?

C *It's all loving energy. If there's damage in any area we all put loving
energy towards repairing the damaged trees, animals and insects. We each*

help nurture and heal. So it's all love. We know that you possess love and respect, but you can feel us and, as it happens, you can also hear us. That's why we wanted you to know more about us.

P Thank you very much.

C It's like I'm holding out my hand to him. So we're all spiritual entities. We're just recognising each other, which we don't often do.

P A point of curiosity for me: as we blunder through the landscape is there damage to the population of nurturing spiritual identities, the devas on the different levels? So even though we blunder through, slipping and sliding, trampling this and treading on that, is what we do of consequence on the spiritual level?

C *We get out of the way. You can't actually damage us. And when an area of bush is destroyed, we move on to somewhere else because it's our habitat too. As has happened with most of this country.*

P So as the bush was destroyed and converted to grassland, what happened to all the innumerable devic carers for the plant and tree populations across this land?

C *You don't so much count us in numbers as in energy, so the energy expands and shrinks as necessary. So it's shrunk. It could extend out to embrace more should it need to. So it's not a question of population. It's not a number. It involves a capacity to shrink and expand.*

P That's interesting. Because, of course, the traditional depiction has always been of individuals.

C *We manifest to you like that. It's easier for you to work out.*

P Okay. It's probably necessary for us to leave quite soon. In terms of the potential for gathering information, is there benefit in returning at a different time? Is there benefit in bringing others who are also sensitive? Or are we sufficient?

C *There is one, the woman Trisha, who would be able to communicate well with us. She is the one who is well-connected and fascinated with us. She may well get some more information.*

P Would you please invite her, then?

C *We recommend waiting until summer. It's not pleasant for humans up here at this time of the year. There's no rush, but she is one who would be—*

P Amply rewarded?

C *Yes.*

P Thank you for clarifying that.

C I haven't come back. If you could hold my hand, that hand, I'll ask it to come back.

[Peter: On the way down the mountain Carolyn stopped, asked to hold my hand in a particular posture, and said the part of her that had gone swooping through the valleys wasn't back with her yet.

Carolyn: I just remember the feeling of absolute confidence and bliss, of being bird-like and in the company of some being. It was like I was accompanying, or had become part of, the energy that toured very high above the mountain and occasionally swooped down the valleys. I also felt part of, or one with, the energy of the plant and animal life there. It was a pretty special feeling!]

P So you responded to the invitation of the mountain deva to leave your body behind and part of you left and went journeying with it? In the interest of your health, well-being and completeness, I ask that part to return now, before we leave this mountain.

C He just said, *It's been a joy to have you with me.*

P Who or what said that?

C The guardian we went on a journey with. It's a big mountain. I've been sailing around it. ... Wow, that's cool. Back again. I'm back!

P Your colour's changed. You were quite pale. How interesting.

C I didn't feel quite comfortable without all of me together. It was a bit odd, actually.

P I dare say.

A tranquil being and an imposter

T Female. Doesn't want to speak. She's ashamed.

K Can you tell us anything about yourself? Do you know where you are? What's the last thing you remember?

I was feeling so bad and so ashamed that I was sure I must have done something really bad. But now you've asked I can't remember what it was. Somehow that makes me feel better.

Do you understand you've passed on?

Not really. Is that why I'm here?

I think so. Do you see the person you're speaking through?

Huh! That's odd.

Can you give us any information about your age, where you were, what you were wearing?

Late forties. It's 1978.

It's 2014 now. Is that a shock?

It's a surprise.

When you look round what do you see?

A thick, grey fog.

Are you alone?

Yes.

Do you feel like it's time to move on?

Can I?

Yes. Look around. Can you see any light? Is the fog dispersing?

I see some light seeping under a door.

See it getting it lighter and larger? Is there someone you're missing who might be on the other side of the door?

The door is open and I can see light, but I'm really not sure I want to go through there. It feels scary.

Light is always a good thing. There's nothing scary there.

I don't see anyone waiting for me.

They will be there, just trust. Are you getting closer?

I'm standing right at the door, peeking through, but I don't see anything.

It doesn't look bad, though?

It's just nothing.

At least it's light. Try and step through.

I don't want to.

Do you have a memory of someone you lost?

My mother.

Can you imagine her waiting for you?

But she'll be so disappointed in me.

That's all in the past. Everyone makes mistakes. We move on.

I think I can see her through there. But I'm so scared.

I'm sure she won't be anything but happy to see you. Imagine her arms reaching out for you.

I have this very strong feeling of fear. It's holding her back. I can't pinpoint what the fear is of.

So she still hasn't gone?

No. She's too scared to go through the door.

C   What if I hold your hand while you step through? Will you come with me? I'll hold your hand, so you're safe.

You're not going to push me through, are you?

No! I'll just hold you. You'll be fine.

I really just need to take that step? What if I regret it?

I've got your hand. You can always step back.

It's fear of doing the wrong thing I think, because she's already done the wrong thing and doesn't want to do the wrong thing again.

There's no such thing as wrong now. Just be brave.

I can see a lot of people now, it looks more welcoming. They seem to want me to go. Okay, I can do it. I'm going to do it.

[Gone.]

T   It was like she was tentatively dipping her toe in water, but as soon as her toe went over to the other side she was suddenly enveloped. Once she was through she looked back at me, as if saying, *Why didn't you tell me? If I'd known it was this good ... !*

P There's a pattern of shame where the person goes into themselves and keeps going over conversations. They can be stuck there a long time.

◊ ◊ ◊

C *I wondered when you were going to get around to me. You've been so busy and ignoring me.*

P You seem to be a little miss, don't you?

A little missed out, I would say!

How old were you, when you died?

Sixteen.

I thought as much. You have the mannerisms of a precocious and obnoxious sixteen year old.

Thank you for that observation.

You're most welcome here. How can we help?

I want to go home.

Where is home for you?

I don't have a home any more. I don't belong where I used to be and I don't know where I am now.

We can give you the best information about where to go next. What do you see around you?

You guys! Hello!

Sharpen your perception, see clearly.

What does that mean?

See clearly.

Just talk clearer! What am I looking for? People? Dogs?

How many people?

Four people, two dogs. D'uh!

What do you see beyond that group?

It's all dark. Just that bright spot.

Get in the middle of that brightest spot. Now look upwards.

Are you guys having a disco or something?

Why?

There's a sparkly, bright shiny mirrored ball thing right up above me. It's lifting up, going up and up. There's a shiny pathway.

Follow it.

Chase the ball?

Yes, it's showing you the way. It will take you home. You'll find people who love you.

Alright. This is quite cool. I'm kind of floating. It's weird. Like a ferris wheel, but going up all the time. Bye!

[Gone.]

◊ ◊ ◊

T A female. Something's happened to her eyes. While Carolyn was talking my head was hanging and my eyes were sore, blind. My head just came back up. She's just realised that she can see again.

P What happened to your eyes?

Did you fix them?

No, you're in a different situation now. You've left your body behind. What do you see, with your new sight?

I see you people.

What else?

It's like everything is flashing before her eyes. There's trees, streets and shops, residential roads, cars. Suddenly, she can see it all.

How long were you blind?

My whole adult life. I never thought I'd see all these things. She's on a safari in Africa now. She's doing everything she ever wanted to see!

There will come a time when you recognise that those things of the Earth are no longer relevant to you. The joy of seeing will be transcended by the joy of being on an entirely different level, where in fact you are now.

I'm in a beautiful flower garden. It's very soothing.

You can expect much more of that tranquillity and quiet joy.

Who's that little guy under the flowers?

I don't know. Ask him. Tell us.

He says you call him the flower tickler! Can everyone see him?
No, almost no one. You could describe him for us, please.
He's quite chubby. He looks very happy snuggling up to the flowers.
Ask him what's the right thing for you to do next.
He says I should listen to you. You know what you're talking about.
Are you willing to do that?
Yes. I think I know. I think it's happening anyway.
[Gone.]

Just before she went my eyes got really sore again, then she was gone and so was the pain.

P I got the impression of acid in the face.

T I get a yes to that. It was really sore.

At this point Karen commented she had a film playing to her mind, showing face after face, but she didn't know what it meant.

P It's possible those are images of you, at other times and places, throughout who knows how many centuries and cultures. It's a download, effectively, which you can replay. Bring it to your conscious awareness. Scribble down what you remember. It's personal information that will give you a clues about the depths of who you are and the nature of your experience, what has shaped you. You're connected to every one by a thread. Across that thread information can come that might surprise you.

◊ ◊ ◊

T My head just got turned all the way round to the right, but at the same level. It stayed like that for a bit, until I said it was making my neck hurt. Then I heard "Oh, sorry!" and my neck straightened out. It's not someone we've met before, but whoever it is happy for us to ask questions. There's an expectant feeling: *Come on!*

P Please define the distinction between us and yourself.

T *I'm not human.*

Then how would you describe yourself?

What do you mean by that?

Are these things you can answer?

I have been human, and now I'm just energy.

So where does that place you on the agapéic frequency scale?

In the FI range. [The group had been discussing the scale before beginning meditation, FI (functional integration) being agapé frequency 35 to 42.]

So that means you are a partially reintegrated identity? How many fragments of Dao- consciousness do you comprise?

Five.

Is it possible to give a percentage figure for reintegration?

80%.

The number five seems anomalous. Can you expand? If there's a better set of parameters, or if that's too restrictive a schema to describe yourself, please use whatever other criteria works for you.

[*Silence.*]

Are they still present, Trisha?

Yes. I just feel like I'm floating.

It might be that the information is coming in a non-verbal way. Perhaps you could articulate what you're experiencing.

The top of my head feels really expanded, elongated. At first it felt like I was being pulled up, but it's more of an expansion. I get the words peaceful and knowing. There's a weightless feeling to it.

Anything indicating freedom to move in that space?

Yes.

Different from your own sense of freedom to move?

Less need to move.

Is that to do with a sense of contentment?

Yes.

So what is the task from this point forward, for them?

To just be.

By what impulse did you arrive to our awareness?

I heard your questions.

Thank you for responding. From your capacity to know, what is it in your perception that you can contribute to our knowing?

Confirmation. I'm seeing those charts. [See graphic on page 137.]

One of the factors that we've been given least information about is regarding where you are manifesting from, in a rightward direction in relation to us, at a higher level of willingness to bequest agapé. Is there any way we can understand more clearly what that means? Is confirmation the essence of the communication?

There is more.

Is our existing concept set adequate, or does it need augmenting?

It needs augmenting.

We would be happy for you to provide such augmentation.

He's gone.

P   That was a particularly subtle and gentle sense of presence. Very tranquil, almost indiscernible, yet there's a space where it was that's empty now. That might be the essence of the information, that somehow there's a quietness, an essential tranquillity, that's different from us. Is there anything you can add to that impression?

T   It just felt very peaceful. Steady, floaty, a suspended feeling. No real need to do anything except be.

No agenda. We've never had anybody quite like that before. I don't understand why they would manifest at this level. Not an identity claiming to have transcended the realm of human incarnation.

Initially my head went straight around to the right. When he was here, he felt higher, like he was hovering.

So quite passively allowing us to sample his presence, then? It might simply be that he only came into our perception when he was already close to us. We have to be careful of our attributions. When you got the impression that it was confirmation, was it confirmation of one part? Or confirmation of the validity of the entire model?

It felt like it was a direct result of us chatting in there before. So it was confirmation of what you'd been saying there in relation to the different realms.

It seemed to me that the identity was completely separate from this group. No shared members, not part of anybody's group soul?

No.

That's independent confirmation then. That's useful.

◊ ◊ ◊

Carolyn comments that she has started feeling very cold.

C *It's not my wish to cause you discomfort! However, it's my way of gaining your attention, seeing as you appear to be dozing off. The previous discussions regarding the observer who was considering space on the agapéic scale ...* This is a visitor who's not familiar with the intricacies of our models. And I wasn't listening to you guys at all, so I'm a bit out of the loop. This is coming from miles away. Maybe you could ask this guy what he's doing?

P Please introduce yourself and how it is you've come to be here.

I've intervened because of the previous questions you were asking. I might be more able to answer them.

From your understanding of our questions, please expand on what we think we know and we observe or lack.

The identity you were speaking to was from the ... you were correct, that part of the scale, FI, it's a stage where ...

[Silence.]

P Just describe it in the words that come as best you can. I know it's not necessarily your habit to think in these analytical ways.

C I have asked the entity who was speaking to you to apologise to you. He's an imposter. He wanted my attention. He just wanted to sit up here and say something.

P So he's not a person of knowledge in the way he claimed to be?

C He was being a smart arse. He's still here. *I just wanted to see if I could, and I did. I just saw you here, and wanted to see if I could get your attention.*

P Well, you have it. What would you like to do now?

I dunno, it just seemed like fun. I don't know what else to do now.

How many other individuals or groups have you interacted with in this way?

I haven't done it before. I just saw you and heard that lady talking with her eyes shut, and thought, I wouldn't mind doing that too.

Where have you been?

Floating around.

Why?

There's nothing else to do.

I presume from your responses that you're human. Is that right?

Course I am.

Then why you don't have a body?

I just don't any more.

Have you got a rational explanation for that?

It's got mangled in a car and a tree. It's a big mess, not pretty.

When and where was that?

Eight months ago. The tree's there, the car's not, and bits of my body got peeled up and stuck in a coffin and stuck in the ground.

You have no idea what to do, have you?

Not really.

Do you want to find out?

Okay, you're the boss.

How many times have you died before?

This is new to me!

I bet it's not the first time.

I'm only seventeen. How many times can you die when you're seventeen!

Depends how many bodies you've had before.

Hello. I was only seventeen. How can I ...

Has nobody ever told you about these things?

No!

Well, you get to have a bunch of bodies, one after the other. As each one dies, you hop off and come back in another.

Oh, that's that reincarnation thing.

That's right. That's the territory you're in the middle of right now.

But that's that eastern bloody philosophical mucking around!

It's actually universal, so pay attention.

Yes, boss.

You get to go to a place that's a bit lighter than it is now. Can you see clearly? What's it like for you?

Well, it's the weirdest thing. It looks like the headlights of a car coming towards me. I better get out the way. But if I haven't got a body I'm not going to get run over, am I?

That's your interpretation. It won't actually be that. What you're seeing will just be partly triggered by your recent experience. Don't be frightened.

It's a bit like a bloody sci-fi movie, but I feel like I'm being sucked towards the lights.

That's all that has to happen. They'll know what to do. That's how you're going to get to the light.

And it's a good thing?

A very good thing. Jump on board and go with them.

My mate is there making a hell of a noise.

Some people have been around a few more times and know what to do. Jump on board and go with him.

There he is. Okay, see ya!

◊ ◊ ◊

P Let's consciously combine our energies and expand the space to include the surrounding countryside and all the life forms in it. Invite them to share and communicate with us, so we can be aware, with greater clarity and understanding, of the nature and purpose of their lives. Allow everything to enter your awareness as you mentally reach through that space. Notice the life forms you encounter, and commune with them for as long seems appropriate, to share your love and desire to know, or to receive theirs.

[Several minutes passed.]

P Retaining that sense of connectedness, bring your attention back into your own body, and lets see who connected to what.

R I went down our drive. There are some big green trees. The oak had some entity or presence. But out front there's a very large tree, and I got the term rogue. It certainly is growing wild and woolly, but I couldn't pick anything inhabiting it or around it.

T I went to the path through our big bush block. I had a feeling of huge energy. It's where the energy of all the elementals meets.

I was asking if we should go there and meditate. I got that that's not necessary, we can just visualise it. There was a feeling of calm. A con-vergence; it was like a huge bubble of energy. It felt different; usually when elementals come to us it's because they're upset about some-thing, but this felt very serene, strong and powerful.

K I went where I normally walk. I could see all the usual animals. Then I was on the back of a hawk, soaring, like a passenger. I felt quite sick after a while and had to stop! Then I was viewing a crowd of people. One particular man was standing out. The others were all shadowed. He kept looking back over his shoulder as he made his way through the crowd. My feet felt like lead.

C I couldn't walk at all, my foot was too sore. It's stopped now, but it was shooting pain. The only thing I thought was, it's time I went dancing again!

P I had a momentary connection with a happy mosquito. I don't equate happiness with mosquitos! Perhaps he was in blissful igno-rance of his end. I made connections with a fish, and an eel, and one of those delicate little flies with transparent wings, and a slug. Little lives.

An observer of humanity

T Who are you?

C *I'm Michael.*

Where are you from?

Around these parts.

What do you do?

Watch out for people like you.

You mean, looking after us? Or just curious about us?

I like to find people I can talk to. There's not many I can talk to, and it gets boring looking after the plants and animals and little people.

That's cool. We like talking to people like you, too.

I know. I've watched you. I wanted to join in. I'm pleased you now know who I am.

Do you have a specific job?

I look after taller trees. Trees in gardens and forests and native bush. I like people who plant trees. Like this lady and her trees.

My husband, who's planting trees?

Yes, they plant trees on the hill. They're very, very important people. I spend a lot of time up there.

That's nice to know. It's nice to be up there.

We like having you there.

Do you have any advice for us?

I'd like to sit down and chat with you sometime. I don't think this is the place, because you have things to do this evening. But I'll come again another day and we'll chat. Maybe sitting under your trees.

That would be cool.

You guys do what you've got to do. I'll come and see you again.

We'll look forward to it.

[Gone.]

T So we have to go meditate in the native garden or bush!

C He is pleased that he's found us, got a communication link to us, and we're going to sit in the trees and talk to him. He's so pleased!

◊ ◊ ◊

T I have a strange feeling on the top of my head, and my face is scrunching in an unusual way. I feel it's a higher being. I get a no to "watching".

P We welcome you. Please communicate your intention.

Now I feel queasy. Like they're looking around at us. Curious.

Please explain your nature and purpose.

I feel like I'm sucking back into myself. If I say "My intent is good" I get no. "My intent is bad" is a yes. I don't have a feeling of maliciousness or anything. They just didn't expect us to notice them.

It's not necessary to react emotionally to the presence of identities who are takers not givers. I'm interested that it manifested on the right-hand side.

Well, sort of above.

Is that the truth? Or the impression conveyed towards you?

The top of my head's really sore now.

Identities of that class are entirely capable of putting up a smoke-screen or disguise. But you can challenge it.

I get yes to "It was a disguise".

This is a very important illustration of what that class of identity is capable of. So not being fooled is the challenge.

What I'm getting is that he's hiding behind me, sucking through me to get behind me.

Pull him out. You can do that.

As soon as I said that the feeling went. Now when I say "He's still here", I get no.

It's appropriate to take command of the situation and hold that class of identity to account. Observe it, and if necessary simply say "take it away". Don't allow those types of identity near you for longer than you wish, no longer than is necessary to satisfy your curiosity and learn what you want to know.

I was waiting to see what would happen. But that's good advice. If it feels at all bad, just tell it to go.

That's one option. Be clear about the character of identity that is present. They have the ability to be wonderful or menacing. But it's all illusion, a sham. Hold one part of your willingness to engage a little separate, and observe critically. Don't get sucked in. One of the things that you can do, as a means of containment, is to instantaneously construct a containment device in the astral realm, and just grab it. I've used enormous cones of entrapment. Just use it to swallow the identity and wrap it tightly, then offer it to those who are on our side. You usually get some response. We don't have to be passive. We can be proactive. It's all very educational.

◊ ◊ ◊

T Oh! I sort of wish I hadn't done that. I thought I would check on that missing airplane and immediately started feeling really queasy. They're all in the sea, trapped. [Trisha felt she was looking at people under a sheet of glass, against which their hands and faces were pressed.]

C We can untrap them. That was a pretty big thing to take on!

T I know! What was I thinking!

R See if there's a spokesperson, someone who can talk for them.

T I'm not sure yet. Can one of you just talk, reassure them, say some nice stuff. Explain what happened.

R It seems the plane you were on has crashed into the sea, and you're no longer alive. You no longer have physical bodies, so you don't need to feel trapped. You can simply move yourself out of there.

We don't know how!

You can simply will your mind, take yourself out.

We don't understand.

If you look at yourselves you'll see you have no bodies. You're now in spirit, and as spirits you can move out of physical things. You've been through a very traumatic experience, but you're no longer in danger or in pain. You can simply move.

Someone is helping us out.

Great. Look around you. Look for a source of light.

We have to get everyone out first.

K You do. Get everyone out. Don't leave anyone behind.

C There's one who wants to stay behind because he doesn't believe in this stuff. He's happy choosing to stay. He believes he had to blow up the plane, so he's not going anywhere.

R Are the others still there? What's happened to them?

C *No. We're all out. What do we do now?*

The next step is that you go towards the light and there will be people there to greet you. Loved ones, people who have passed on before you. Look around. Look up.

K Is anyone still in the water?

C No.

R Look for a source of white light and expect to see people coming to greet you. Take yourselves towards the light.

We're going. We're all holding hands and we're going.

That's a great way to go.

[Gone.]

C Karen, could you hold my hand. This guy is still here.

K Can I talk to you? I have no understanding of why or how, but whatever you did you must have believed. You now need to move on too. There must have been some purpose, some reason why you were driven to do what you did. But you'll never work through it unless you also leave the wreck. Face whatever comes. It can't be as bad as where you are. You must have seen the others go?

R You don't need to go to the same place.

K Tell me what you're feeling?

C It's just black.

K Your heart? Or the surroundings?

The surroundings, black and heavy. How are you going to lift this out of these depths?

When you were alive, what gave you the most joy? Someone? Something? Family?

He's melted in the love. It's melted all the black.

Is he moving? He just needs to hold that thought of the most joyful thing that he can remember.

He's lifted to another place.

T   When I saw all the people coming out, and lifting up to the light, it was like the last person went, and he was left there strapped in his seat just plummeting to the bottom of the ocean.

C   Yes, just heavy and yuk. Another opening of love came in from somewhere else, and the tar, glue and horribleness just melted. He didn't have any choice but to be lifted up. He was almost yanked up, almost unwilling. Love pulled him up.

R   Did he have a bomb on board?

C   That's the feeling I had. He felt righteous. My hand has been shaken by that guy.

R   What does that signify?

C   He thanks us. The evil thing he did, he was rescued in spite of it. He's amazed we know what he did and we don't hate him. He's been taught to hate. He doesn't any more.

◊ ◊ ◊

T   Someone else is here. My head is getting bobbled about all over the place. It's not a spirit, not human.

R   Welcome to you. How may we be of service?

T   *What are you offering?*

Love and respect and goodwill, and the opportunity to talk if you wish to tell us about yourself.

[Shrugs.] *Tell me about you.*

We are a group of humans who meet to meditate and place ourselves in a position to be of service to those in spirit.

Well, I don't know that I need your help, but it's pleasant to be here. I could hang out with you.

You're most welcome. Would you tell us a little about yourself?

What's to say? [Trish feels Jewish mannerisms and shrugs.]

P What are the archetypes that you identify with?

T When I say "I am Jewish" I get a yes.

R Were you once a human?

No.

What form of spirit are you?

That's a good question. I don't really know. I just am.

You've come from a group, or are you a solitary individual?

From a group.

What's the nature of the group?

C Do you work with humans and help them?

T *We're peaceful.* I get a no to "help humans". I see them in robes. They're not angels.

R What is your purpose?

We observe.

What do you do with your observations?

We report to the Higher Council.

T They have good intent, not bad. I think they're observing human beings in their current lives and reporting to the Higher Council how they cope with what happens to them.

R Why does the Higher Council want to know how humans are coping?

T *The information is used when advising them about the choices they have for their next life.*

So this is like an advisory council helping people?

When they come back to the light, the Council knows what's been going on. They can discuss it with them and help them make choices.

P Is this an independent assessment channel, through you? Independent of human feedback?

Yes.

That's important for quality control.

Yes. We don't interfere.

R Is one of your kind assigned to each human, or do you observe groups of humans?

Groups.

P Are you associated with the group soul level of any particular group, or are you independent of that too?

Independent. We don't watch anyone twenty-four hours a day. We just dip in and out.

P Historically there's been a group called the Great White Brotherhood. What's the relationship between that and the Higher Council you're describing?

The Great White Brotherhood is us. But you're not supposed to know that.

Thank you for that clarification. And your trust.

Don't tell anyone else.

Are you really serious when you say that?

Within your group is fine, but you shouldn't tell just anybody.

I don't think they'd understand, anyway. Most people have no idea about the Great White Brotherhood, either its history or the extensive literature about it. But I would like to have a greater understanding of what you do.

Haven't I been clear?

I'm a little confused. You said "the Great White Brotherhood is us". Does that mean you as observer, rather than the Higher Council? Is that what you meant?

Yes.

So the perception and the naming of that Great White Brotherhood is a mistake? Or just terminology from another time?

The common perception is a mistake.

In relation to the approximately nearly seven billion humans resident on this planet, how many are you?

Thousands, not hundreds of thousands.

Which implies one per million people, or thereabouts? That's a big surveillance set. You must be busy.

Some need more attention than others.

Is it possible for you to describe in any more detail the activities of the Higher Council?

I'm not privy to that.

Is there anything else appropriate for you to share with us now?

Keep up the good work.

Thank you very much. Would you inform the identity whose voice you are using why she felt a connection to a Jewish nature of some kind? I'm just wondering whether it was part of your inquisitiveness, or something else?

T Something else. When I say, "her sense of our Jewishness was correct", I get a yes. But I'm not getting anything much. All I get is peaceful.

P What is the relationship between you, Trisha, and that identity? Are you one of his observed set?

T No. Carolyn is. But he came to observe all of us. He feels male. The visual is very male. Men in white or cream robes.

R So you saw a number of individuals, but only spoke to one?

T Yes. The others were standing behind him.

P I think that's the first connection we've had to that class of identity, and of reference to the Higher Council in those terms. We've never had anything so explicit before.

A moss minder and a farm supervisor

P   I feel I'm surrounded by small people. They're not human. They're full of joy and curiosity. They're manifesting on my right side and to the left.

T   I seem to have an elemental with me, but I'm not getting any particular feeling or emotion.

P   The crowd of little elementals that were here all evaporated away. Would it be okay to invite your visitor to introduce itself?

T   I don't think he knows why he's here. When I asked, "Is there some way we can help you?", my eyes started darting right and left, as if "Where am I?", "Can you see me?", "Are you talking to me?"

P   Yes, we are. We have curiosity and goodwill, and seek to learn about individuals such as yourself. Could you answer some questions?

There's nothing to know about me!

I appreciate you might think so, but from our perspective it's a very rare experience for us to encounter an individual such as yourself. We know very little about your kind of being, so could you please share everything you can about your existence and activities?

I look after the moss on the trees.

Very good. I'm glad someone does that. We've never met anybody who looks after moss before. Can you describe how you look after it?

Just by being near it and giving it good energy. Sometimes I talk to it.

Do you feel that it understands you?

It seems to like that.

How does it respond to the feelings that you have and the communication that you have?

It makes it happy and healthy.

How does it do that?

I don't know. It's just good energy.

Okay. Does it need your attention all the time? Or more sometimes than others?

I cover a big area so I check back and make sure everything's okay.

How do you feel in summer when there's very little moisture, the sun is strong, and the moss dries out?

It's as it should be.

So there's nothing wrong?

No. There's still damper areas in the bush.

I seem to sense an identity that has come present, and is looking at you, or looking at Trisha. Who is that, do you know?

I don't see anyone else.

It's not an elemental.

I only see you people.

You do see us?

Yes. I don't know how I got here, but I can see you.

What do we look like to you? Have you met humans before?

No. They're quite big, aren't they? Bigger than me.

How does our energy feel to you?

Compatible. I've seen humans before, just never spoken to them.

Where is your patch that you look after? Is there a way that you can describe that to us?

This patch of bush, between the Woolshed and the ponds.

Have you seen Trisha before?

Yes, I saw her this afternoon.

Does it make any difference, since you haven't previously spoken to humans, knowing that you've seen her and you know how she feels?

She seems non-threatening.

What would something threatening feel like? Have you met anyone like that?

Not for a long time.

Can you measure your age?

No.

You don't count seasons or anything like that?

We don't count them. I'm aware of them because of what I do.

Are you aware of the impact of the day, the sun, the night, and rain, on the moss, the changes of climate?

Yes.

But you don't think about conditions this year as being different from last year?

Does that matter? It is what it is. I can't change it.

Have you always been present in this place, where you are now?

I was somewhere else before. This century in human terms. I moved from next door, but I like it better here.

Was that your choice?

Yes.

Why did you move?

Energy.

So you felt drawn here?

Yes.

There was a need that you responded to?

There's always a need.

Had there been anyone else here before you?

Not when I came. Not everywhere is covered. We go where there is choice. We like to be happy.

What is it that makes you feel that this is a better place than where you were before?

They look after us here.

Who does?

The humans.

How do they do that?

They take care of the land.

Is that what feels better?

Yes.

Their attitude, their actions?

Yes.

What would be taking care of the land worse?
Chopping down my trees.
That would be disturbing, I expect.
Not knowing that we're even there, not caring.
Are you happy that Trisha knows that you're there?
Yes.
Does Ian [Trisha's husband.] know that you're there?
He doesn't think like that, but he does the right things.
One of those things would be planting more trees?
Yes.
R What is your precise function there?
Looking after the moss.
C Was there somebody looking after the moss here before you chose to come here?
Not when I came.
So there was no moss minders here before?
No. Not in that area.
So not all areas have moss minders?
No. If there's bad energy nobody wants to be there.
What happened to the place you moved from? Did someone else come?
No.
What constitutes bad energy? What's its source?
The person looking after the land.
Are there any other ways that you can explain what kind of energy feels bad to you?
Sterile land, bad farmers. The ones who don't think about the land.
Does that mean they think about the animals, but not the land the animals graze on?
I don't know about animals.
R Sometimes farmers do things that change the nature of the soil, and it means moss doesn't grow there any more, perhaps only in shady places. Is this the sort of thing that you mean? Or is it more the attitude of the farmers who don't manage the land and allow erosion?

Yes, the attitude. The farmers with that energy don't have many trees.

P You seem to know something of that sort of farmer.

Where I was before.

Trees were cut down, the land dried out?

It didn't feel right. It wasn't a nice place to live.

How do you perceive those kinds of feelings from the land owner?

T I have a picture of a farmer on a quad bike, with a ripple, a wave of bad energy, emanating out.

You don't want to be near that.

Like a local atmosphere around him?

It affects everything.

Is that because they seek to exploit the land?

Yes.

Does that mean they're people who are not intrinsically loving?

I don't know about that.

T The feeling I get from him is that that's outside his experience. He doesn't know how humans feel.

[Gone.]

◊ ◊ ◊

T I have the feeling that someone else has been present.

P I have a sense of a taller entity over on the right, vaguely columnar, maybe like a tree trunk.

R Perhaps he brought the deva.

P That was an example of a species specific elemental, not a supervisory level. Now I have a feeling somebody else is around who would like to say something, but I'm not quite sure of the identity.

T It's another elemental.

P It's whizzing around underneath us, perhaps to decide which of us to latch on to.

T I think it's me because it's making me feel sick. It's like figure eights for some reason.

P Is it flying around like that because that's what it does?

T I got a yes to "This is what I do."

P But why?

It just is. It's my job.

Who benefits from your job? What are you attending to?

I have to keep an eye on everything.

Are you a supervisor?

Yes.

I'm very pleased to meet you. What is your territory?

This farm and not outside that.

So you respect human boundaries?

Yes. The energy changes on the other side of the fence.

Is there anything that you would like to tell the person you are speaking through about her farm? What they're doing that's right, and what they could do more of, so that you'd feel even better?

They're doing okay.

Do you have any advice for them?

No. They're doing the right things.

Do you feel it's a good idea for you to chat to Trisha at any time? Are you available for that, if she were to enquire?

I'm quite busy.

I understand that. I just imagine that if there could be good communication at least between you and Trisha perhaps you could establish a conscious level working partnership. Would that be of interest?

I haven't done that before. I could contact her if something wasn't right.

You might find you have ideas which she might want to know, how to make it better for the different plants and trees, and all the other species on their farm which is your patch.

I think my people should go to her direct. I need to just look after them.

Okay. How would they know to do that? Could you tell them?

I can tell them. That's okay. The moss guy will tell them.

Did you bring that guy?

No, he brought me. He didn't seem to know how he came to be here. I don't know how he came to be here, but he told me maybe I should come too.

If he didn't come from his idea, whose idea was it? Is there some higher level that we can access to explain this?

I feel a bit worried. I don't know how it happened.

I'm sure you don't need to worry about it. It might be that there's a level that is concerned with maybe the whole hill, not just the property. Do you think that might be true? It sounds like it's not something you know about. I certainly don't mean to worry you.

These are my people.

I'm not suggesting there's anything wrong at all.

R It's a very positive thing that the moss guy and you have come and talked to us. Very useful and positive.

I don't need to be worried about it?

I don't think so.

T When he was worried he stopped buzzing around and was still. Now he's back to buzzing around again!

R I get the feeling of a very fragile kind of being, in an emotional sense.

[Gone.]

P The energy very distinctly changed just then, with his anxiety.

T I felt on the elemental's behalf like there was a presence. I didn't know what it was and it was a concern to me.

P It felt like something significantly higher responsibility.

R It was obviously beyond that entity's experience and view. He's in this little area with the territory he has to look after. He doesn't know what else is above him.

P I'm very interested in establishing a link or access to that broader supervisory level, if that's possible, and exploring the responsibility and interests it has, finding out how expansive its territory would be.

T When I was buzzing around I felt like I was literally looking at every corner of the farm. I paused next to some big old natives, a couple of which aren't thriving, and I found myself thinking *I'll need to keep an eye on that one.*

P Was there any feeling for the range of sub-species under that one's view? Was it everything, all the species, all plants, all animals? Or just some subset of it?

T Not animals, but all plants. It did include grass and soil and all kinds of plants, trees, but not animals. I think that means just not farm animals.

P So it might be soil animals?

T Yes. But not insects.

P I have the impression of looking out over broad landscapes, to far horizons, with lots of land forms within view. A sense of really broad territory, coast to coast, as if having a vantage point up above the clouds. Really serene, unconcerned with the detail. As if the North Island might be one territory and the South Island another territory, some sort of supervisory oversight on that scale. Where a mountain erupting would be of minor interest. On a scale of concern where the inroads made by humans are a recent and short term event. Maybe it's a purview of hundreds of centuries and comprises another element in the spiritual hierarchy of responsibility for this particular planet. No commentary at all, just the opportunity to briefly look out through his eyes.

R So each land mass could have its own minder?

P It looks that way.

Epilogue

The following material was channelled by Peter Calvert a month before the meditation encounters presented here. A statement by the
guides, it offers a context for why the encounters with elementals
matter, and also points to a fundamental issue that humanity needs
to address.

It is important to remember that every species without exception has its atten-
dant spiritual associate, and for a very good reason. That reason is to gather
information directly from the fields of activity experienced by the members of
that species. Each spiritual associate's purpose is to direct appropriate chang-
es within the ecological niche. By processing the flow of information within a
niche, and responding by updating its design, spiritual associates help trans-
form a local environment so it remains stable over extended periods.

In this way, spiritual associates help sustain self-modulating, self-devel-
oping communities of species. From the broad perspective, these communities
are interlinked, each interacting with others. Over time, as population pres-
sures build, the spiritual associates respond to these pressures in positive and
negative ways, which in turn supports the flow of energy and nutrients be-
tween the interlinked communities. Hence a complex web of life is sustained.

The stability of the web of life is the long-term goal of the spiritual as-
sociates of all species on this planet. Naturally, perturbations occasionally
arise, for a variety of reasons. In the past changes in the environment were
most common. Today human-caused perturbations are occurring on a global
scale. As a consequence, humanity has an opportunity to observe and analyse
the disturbances they are generating in order to understand what is taking
place, then to cooperatively address their conclusions.

The principal issue now, of course, is the spread of the human population across the planet and the consequent changes in environmental conditions, to the extent that human activities now impact on almost all non-human species. Consequently, human beings have the responsibility of identifying the environmental changes they have initiated and developing policies to counter them.

Many kinds of response are possible. However, no compulsion applies. Human beings may choose to act or not. Naturally, before action comes awareness, and the bulk of the human population either remains unaware of what is occurring or chooses not to seriously respond. In that sense, the bulk of life on the planet is currently being held to ransom by the surge in its human population.

Occasionally, a planet attains this level of dominance by one species. A variety of choices are available, depending on the species' biology, self-awareness and goodwill. Changes invariably need to be adopted long-term, with awareness of the detail and magnitude of what is required resulting in memes being generated within the population. However, resistance to change is also typical. The magnitude of concern that needs to be generated, and the extent of changes needed to reverse current conditions, chiefly by rebalancing relative population levels, are such that disharmony and discontent among many sub-groups within the human population is inevitable.

A prerequisite to change is establishing effective communication between all affected parties. We note that on this planet technology to facilitate communication is available, although not equally and not to everyone. In addition, communication is hampered by the way knowledge is dispersed, and how it is slanted by different communities. One result is the distrust directed by less developed communities towards the more developed. This emanates from long-existing concerns regarding imbalances between them, allied to pressures on their own communities' survival. This is why not only is widespread resistance to change inevitable, but subsequent environmental, economic and political instablitity will likely lead to resource wars.

Accordingly, we consider some centuries will yet pass before a well-informed subset of the human population will accumulate sufficient wisdom to address the situation and communicate successfully that individuals need to voluntarily participate in limiting human fecundity. Therefore be under no illusion that what we say to you, and through you, will have any impact in the short term. That is vanishingly improbable!

Nevertheless, our hope is that reason will eventually prevail. In asserting this we add our voice to those already raised regarding these matters. However, we point out that efforts made by concerned individuals will need to be redoubled if a truly effective response is to be generated, sufficient to prevent the demise of large numbers of species that have developed over thousands of millennia. At the same time, we acknowledge it is pointless raising these concerns within impoverished populations starved of the necessities of life, who have inadequate food, inadequate water, and inadequate shelter against, in many instances, harsh and unforgiving climates.

So a balance is required, both within human communities and beyond human communities, a balance grounded in an informed understanding of all that is involved. Central to this understanding is an appreciation of the need to establish a natural balance between humanity as resource consumer and humanity as resource contributor, which in turn involves appreciating that non-human species have an equal right to exist and propagate beside the human species, and that therefore the human population will need to be limited to ensure all other species have an equal opportunity to survive. Only then can there be confidence that equilibrium will be restored in the web of life, of which the human species is a part. We decline to put a number on the size of the human population required to sustain such an equilibrium, except to indicate that it is a fraction of the contemporary population.

As we stated, humanity is unlikely to respond decisively to this situation for several centuries. Yet that does not preclude an enthusiastic, even vigorous, attending to these issues, including raising at political levels the matter of human culpability for worldwide environmental change. Which has begun. Observing, mapping and predicting species population declines will provide a template for action to guide future global decision-makers. They do not yet exist, nor will for some time. Nonetheless, we add our voice to this expression of concern and, we hope, this communication will provide another level of context, beyond the purely physical and biological, within which such change can be understood.

Appendices

The following models and their accompanying explanations are intended to provide a context so readers may understand how the mediators interacted with non-embodied identities. They also provide a frame of reference for appreciating the varieties of their natures. All models have been provided by Peter Calvert's guides. The accompanying explanations have been channelled.

Human beings' alternative sensory apparatus

A sensory system facilitates the absorption of information. Without a means of receiving information, an individual would be unable to receive any input from its environment. Biologically, the primary uses of any body's sensory system is to find food, avoid danger, find shelter and interact with a mate for the continuation of the species.

For human beings, their body's senses enable them to interact with their local environment, extracting information so they may avoid danger, find food, and so on. Of course, human beings are a more complex biological entity than most other species on this planet, having a central nervous system and brain that facilitate layered cognitive processing. They enable human beings to process complex social, emotional and intellectual information, and make possible intricate interactions that have little to do with survival and food gathering. All this is well documented in the reports of medical, neurological, psychological and anthropological studies.

However, what is much less documented is humanity's alternative sensory system. This system is hinted at by the terms sixth sense and ESP, but how it functions is scantily understood. Much discussion of this alternative sensory system is mired in vague terminology and illustrative metaphors that have little relevance in today's world. It is possible to be much clearer, and more straightforward, in describing how humanity's alternative sensory system functions.

In simple terms, it may be said that the alternative sensory system utilises the aura. However, the aura is itself another much misunderstood and maligned term, its functioning being overstated at times by enthusiastic progenitors and its existence peremptorily rejected by deniers. Accordingly, a brief description of its nature is required.

Biological entities do not have just a material existence, involving flesh, bones and chemicals. Biological entities also possess an electromagnetic dimension. Electrical impulses are crucial to the flow of information through all living entities. That information-carrying

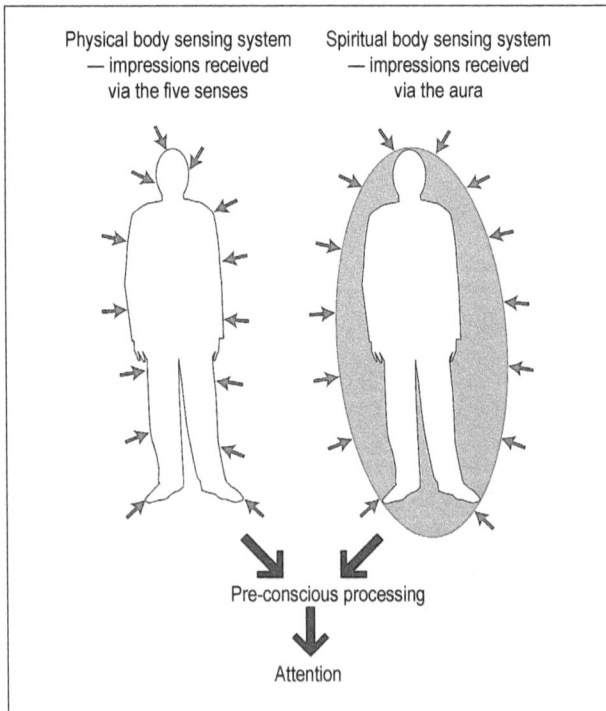

Physical body sensing system
— impressions received
via the five senses

Spiritual body sensing system
— impressions received
via the aura

Pre-conscious processing

Attention

electrical impulses jump between synapses in the human brain is well known. But this is just one aspect of a human body's electromagnetic dimension. In addition, biological entities also have an electrical field, which may be measured by sensors placed just above the skin, bark or other forms of epidermis. This is not in dispute, having been scientifically verified. Less widely known is that every biological entity also possesses an energetic envelope that extends far beyond the epidermis. Kirlian photography has been used to record this. Because, in the case of human beings, the energetic envelope surrounds the body in an oval shape, it was named the aura long ago by those who perceived it, and the name has since stuck.

The aura has several purposes. Of relevance to the encounters presented here is that it serves as an alternative sensory system. It is via the aura that non-incarnate beings are perceived and non-physical forms of information are received. So it is via their auras that the meditators were able to communicate with non-embodied identities, as recorded in this book. In effect, the aura functions as an interface between the spiritual identities and the meditators' everyday minds, which are centred on their physical brains and which receive non-physical communications when they give them attention.

One further point needs to be made regarding the way information passes from the spiritual level, through the aura, to the everyday mind. This is that the everyday mind contains a layer of *preconscious processing*. *Preconscious processing* refers to concepts and assumptions embedded in the receiver's mind. In most cases they are learned, being placed there during childhood through education and enculturation. These pre-existing concepts and assumptions are used to interpret, and as a result they colour, all information an individual receives.

The impact of preconscious processing is clearly seen in the traditional depiction of nature spirits as fairies and gnomes. What happens is that when an individual perceives via their aura that a non-embodied spiritual identity is present, and they use their everyday mind to pay attention to that perception, the mind's pre-conscious processing reshuffles the perception into the form of a fairy or gnome. The non-embodied identity has no such form. The form of fairy or gnome is a human interpretation, a projection laid over the top of the received information, transforming it so it is perceived as being consistent with human pre-conceptions. The identity exists, but the individual's perception of the identity has been impacted by pre-processing. Naturally, having perceived a fairy or gnome, the individual concludes that the traditional view is correct, that nature spirits really do take the form of fairies and gnomes. We assert this is incorrect. All the person has confirmed is the powerful hold cognitive pre-conscious processing shaped by traditional notions has on human perception.

What can those receiving such perceptions do about their mistaken processing? The first step is to appreciate that pre-conscious processing occurs. The second is to be aware that the mind projects its assumptions onto all arriving information, whether that information arrives via the body's sensory system or via the aura's sensory system. Third, everyone is advised to question their assumptions, because human beings project their assumptions onto the world continuously.

By way of an example of human projection, it is commonly said that having a positive or negative outlook colours your view of life, as is encapsulated in the homily that people see a glass half-filled with water as either half full or half empty. This is supposed to indicate whether a person is an optimist or a pessimist. While such a conclusion is open to question, this example does indicate that an individual's psychological make-up colours their interpretation of sensory input. This innate psychological tendency is then augmented by education, which shapes conceptual presets within the mind. In the case of the example, the observer's educational pre-sets define water and glass, while psychological make-up decrees it is half full or half empty.

The impact of education is also seen in the way that religious instruction colours a person's interpretation of non-embodied identities, while a scientific education leads to such perceptions being excluded or, if inadvertently perceived, to their being dismissed as imagined. All this needs to be appreciated when deciding what has actually been perceived via the aura.

The principal advice we offer is that your understanding of what is happening around you in spiritual terms is not enhanced by automatically questioning the validity of perceptions received via your aura, nor by rejecting out of hand that category of input. However, do be aware that pre-conscious processing almost certainly colours your perceptions. Becoming aware of your personal pre-set notions and assumptions will help limit the extent to which you project learned attitudes and notions onto auric-level information received during meditation.

A model of agapéic space

Agapéic space refers to the spiritual domain meditators enter during meditation. When meditators close their eyes, still their minds, and "look out" into the mental void, they project their awareness into a spiritual dimension we are naming agapéic space.

The word *agapéic* derives from the ancient Greek, *agapé*, meaning brotherly love. The term was later adopted by Christians to refer to spiritual love. The spiritual domain may be called agapéic space because human beings are able to consciously access it via love. As the meditator's records show, not all spiritual beings are motivated by love or are able to access it in the way human beings do.

This is not to slight non-human spiritual identities, because they have other facets to their identity that don't apply to the human. This reflects the diversity of spiritual identities, which differ in innate attributes, abilities and capacities in the same way that the biological species on this planet differ, sometimes enormously. Biological species diversity is seen in locomotion—flying, walking, swimming, leaping, boring, drifting—and in the various ways that species eat, reproduce, communicate, share, perceive and process perceptions. Spiritual identities are diverse to a similar degree.

Human beings like to consider themselves the pinnacle against which all else is measured, so rate other creatures in relation to themselves. From the widest perspective, this is an entirely arbitrary way to rate other beings. From a biological perspective, different species are merely different. None is intrinsically higher or lower, superior or inferior. Similarly, from a spiritual perspective, different varieties of identity are not higher or lower, superior or inferior. They are merely different.

That means the variety of spiritual identity that inhabits human bodies, a variety we suggest is fundamentally driven by love, is neither superior to, nor inferior to, other varieties of spiritual identities that are driven by other imperatives, such as a need to expand their wisdom, or to expand the diversity of their perceptions, or to willingly embrace a solitary traveller's existence.

Accordingly, we propose that human beings are driven by a fundamental need to develop their capacity to love. As a result, their development may be measured in these terms. This is reflected in a developmental scale we term agapéic frequency.

The model of agapéic frequency

Agapéic frequency denotes a willingness to act from love. We propose a scale of agapéic frequency that extends from zero to sixty-five thousand. [See the following graphic.] These are notional numbers only, from which we have generated a model to indicate the nature of human awareness within the extension of all agapéic (spiritual) space. What is readily apparent is that human capacities occupy a very small range within the totality of what is possible.

That human capacities occupy a small range will come as no surprise to those who have explored the traditional notions of God, which is conceived as being far vaster and more extensive than the human soul. However, we consider the terms God and soul to be among the concepts that have become so overloaded with diverse and often contradictory meanings that using them impacts detrimentally on individual's investigations of their spiritual capacities. Accordingly, we do not use either God or soul in our models, and suggest that those who seek to explore their spiritual nature are best to situate both concepts among the pre-sets that unduly colour their processing of auric-level perceptions and that they therefore set them aside.

Willingness to act from love produces hierarchy. The term hierarchy, in the sense we are using it here, is not the same as the social hierarchy promoted in human cultures. Socially, hierarchy denotes one person being above another, whether by virtue of occupation, wealth, heredity or celebrity. Instead, we use the term hierarchy in the sense of progression, a developmental progression. Agapéic hierarchy doesn't result in one person being inherently more spiritual than another. It merely denotes their greater capacity to love.

Hierarchy, then, constitutes the sum and product of loving acts enacted throughout a life. It reflects an individual's incrementally increasing willingness to act lovingly towards others. Hierarchy increases as an individual undergoes a wide variety of testing experiences, then evaluates what was done lovingly in a life and what was not. The individual consequently reformulates its inner nature with the goal of eventually becoming willing to act from agapé in any and all situations, towards any and all beings. As an individual becomes more willing and able to act from love there is an increase in agapéic frequency.

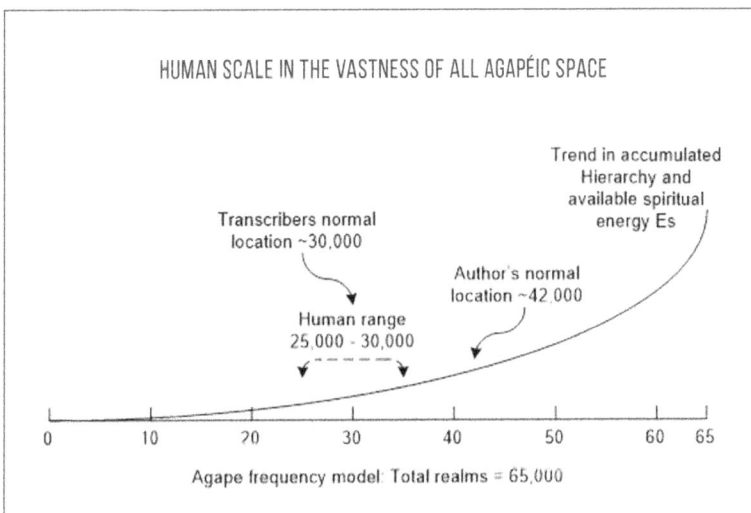

HUMAN SCALE IN THE VASTNESS OF ALL AGAPÉIC SPACE

Transcribers normal location ~30,000

Trend in accumulated Hierarchy and available spiritual energy Es

Author's normal location ~42,000

Human range 25,000 - 30,000

0   10   20   30   40   50   60   65

Agape frequency model: Total realms = 65,000

This has ramifications for meditators when they seek to enter agapéic space.

When a meditator enters agapéic space

When inexperienced meditators first enter agapéic space in order to interact with whatever makes itself known in the spiritual domain, there is some advantage to paying attention to the direction from which activities, presences or impulses arrive into the awareness.

First, the individual needs to be open perceptually. This is achieved by activating the brow chakra and extending perception via that energetic node. Next meditators should visualise themselves as being within a three-dimensional zone of existence. When individuals tune into the agapéic level by directing their focused attention via the brow chakra, they become aware of a very large perceptual space in which they themselves are located, as if in the middle of the sky.

One way for those inexperienced in this type of perception to accustom themselves to spiritual level input is to imagine their body boarding a plane, the plane taking off, flying high into the sky, and entering a cloudy space. There imagine, within that cloudy space, the

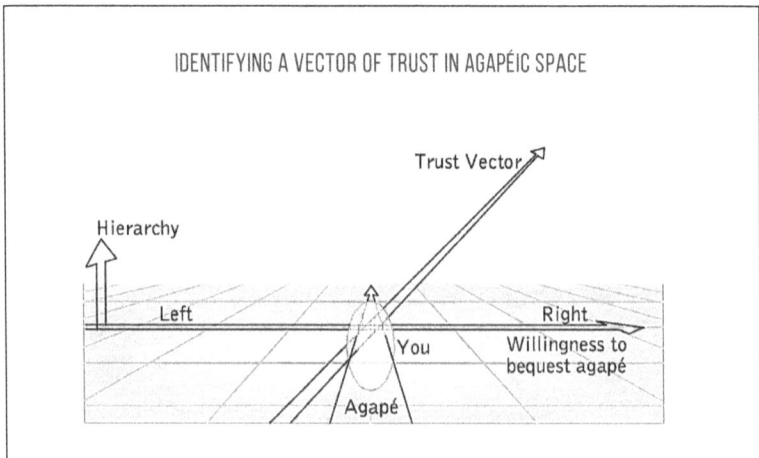

IDENTIFYING A VECTOR OF TRUST IN AGAPÉIC SPACE

Trust Vector

Hierarchy

Left

Right

You

Willingness to
bequest agapé

Agapé

plane stopping, but not falling. Then picture the plane dissolving, or disappearing, or falling out of the mental picture, leaving the individual suspended and stationary, experiencing only that cloudy space.

That is the perceptual analogue of what is experienced when individuals directly perceive themselves being within spiritual space. There is nothing around them. They are present but going nowhere, and they cannot see anything. In fact, commonly there is no perceptual input via the brow chakra.

Initially, it is as if there is no light in that cloudy space. Therefore the fog seems to be black, or at least very dull, and no matter how much the meditator tries little is seen. However, if the meditator spends enough time in that initial condition, being content to direct their attention via the appropriate perceptual channel, with practice that door of perception can be cleaned, as it were, and eventually the meditator becomes aware of being suspended in agapéic space observing the variety of movements of individuals in proximity. This is because others present in that domain eventually recognise the meditator as being an object of interest, with whom communication may potentially be made.

The direction of proximate individuals carries information about their relative status, in spiritual terms, as regards their willingness to bequest love. A general vector may be drawn between those higher in relative agapé frequency and hierarchy and those lower in relative frequency and hierarchy. This vector, relative to the meditating individual, thus proceeds upwards into the forward-right quadrant and downwards into the rear-left quadrant. [See accompanying graphic.]

Those who come from the upper right are invariably trustworthy. Those who come from the lower left rear quadrant may or may not be trustworthy. Those who move with apparent freedom in the generally forwards direction may be doing so as a test of the individual's perceptual capacity to track their movements. And those who rise up from the lower rear left quadrant are generally to be greeted with loving goodwill while maintaining alert awareness with regard to their energetic signature.

It must be noted that this model has been generated to help the meditating human being appreciate differences in the natures of those they interact with in agapéic space. So it is entirely a human-level concept. Once an individual's body dies, and their awareness is no longer tied to the physical domain, these references become obsolete and other frames of reference apply. In other words, this is a model developed specifically for the embodied human awareness.

Varieties of identities on the agapé scale

As the meditators' experiences make clear, spiritual identities are associated with all biological species on the Earth, as well as with every ecosystem and environmental niche. This being the case, it is useful to identity the range of those identities as they exist on this planet. Accordingly, we offer a model we are calling agapé scale. The purpose of this scale is to create a conceptual framework human investigators may use to conceptually order those identities relative to each other.

The scale extends from 0 to 65,000. As with agapéic frequency, these are arbitrary numbers, generated for illustrative purposes only. We note that as with the concept of agapéic hierarchy, no sense of higher or lower, greater or smaller is intended by this scale. This scale may be likened to identifying the size difference between an oak tree and a daisy. A single oak tree is larger, and so has the capacity to absorb more sunlight, rain and minerals than can a single daisy. Yet one is not more important or greater than the other. They each have their place within the ecosystems they occupy. The same applies to identities situated on the agapé scale.

Before beginning, we clarify that this scale refers not to the biological species themselves but to the spiritual identities who associate with various species. For those that associate with plants we accord the range of 5 to 10. [*The numbers used here have a multiplier of 1,000.*]

Spiritual identities that co-exist with group or hive minds, for instance, vertebrates such as aquatic species, avian species, and nests of social insects such as bees and ants, exist in the range of between 10 and 15 on the agapéic frequency scale. We also place invertebrates such as worms, and those with exoskeletons, such as crustacea, within this range of nodes.

Spiritual identities that co-associate with warm-blooded mammals we place on a scale of 15 to 20.

Elementals, those non-embodied identities that oversee vegetation and environmental niches, we situate from 20 to 25.

Spiritual identities that co-associate with human bodies extend across a range from 25 to 35. By this we mean that when an inexperienced identity first associates with a human body it is at 25 on the agapéic frequency scale. As it matures, its agapéic frequency increases. When it reaches 35 on this scale, and when it also achieves maturity on the other two axes [agapéic hierarchy and willingness to bequest agapé], it graduates from the incarnation cycle and rejoins other fragments at the same developmental stage who are beginning the process of reintegrating the fragments into a reunified whole. [For an explanation of this process see the following comments on fragments of Dao-consciousness.]

The spiritual identities that co-associate with the cetacean family

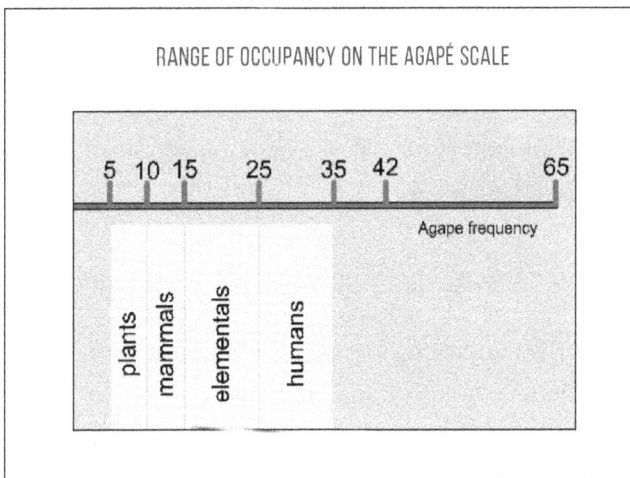

RANGE OF OCCUPANCY ON THE AGAPÉ SCALE

5 10 15   25   35 42   65

Agape frequency

plants mammals elementals humans

of whales, dolphins and porpoises extend from 20 to 30. So there is an overlap with humanity that makes it possible for node fragments of this complexity to migrate to human experience, although not many choose to do so due to the demands the human body and human interactions place on them. It is more common for identities co-associating with the human species to spend time among the cetaceans. Although even this is infrequent, as most of those rare individuals who seek an alternative body form and social experience select species from other planets.

Note that, like the human, there is a frequency range for the identities that associate with various forms of physical life. As with the human, this range indicates a developmental scale. That is, identities begin co-association at the lowest point in the range of agapéic frequency and as they mature they progress to the highest point within that range. They then graduate from embodiment.

We situate ourselves, as a reintegrated node of Dao-consciousness, at 42 on this scale. Given that we were once embodied node fragments, and that we have previously progressed from 25 to 35, what this model implies is that nodes of Dao-consciousness are not limited in their evolution. As they experience and learn, so they themselves expand their capacity, in most cases to a radical extent, compared to their naive and inexperienced state when first cast from the Dao. Hence this scale applies only to nodes during their cycle of co-associating with a physical species. They all grow beyond that.

The range beyond 42 we will not discuss as this is not our brief in relation to this transmission.

Dao-consciousness, nodes and fragmentation

To replace the traditional concepts of God and soul, which as we observed have become overused and outworn, we propose the terms of Dao-consciousness, nodes and fragments.

Dao is the Ultimate Unmanifest. Everything that exists comes from the Dao. This includes all spiritual identities, which we here name nodes of Dao-consciousness. This is because consciousness, along with intent, is intrinsic to the Dao and derives from it.

The Dao's nature is to manifest nodes. Nodes are individual agglomerations of consciousness that are cast from the Dao—by "cast from the Dao" we refer to the spontaneous natural development of a node that consists of the same substance as the Dao. Of course, the term substance is false, for the nature of the Dao has no substance in a conventional sense. So a node of Dao-consciousness may be thought of as a spontaneously agglomerated product of Dao-nature.

Each node of Dao-consciousness may be likened to a droplet. Like droplets, nodes consist of various magnitudes and complexity. We will discuss the significance of nodal magnitude and complexity presently. But first we need to discuss what happens to a node when it initially becomes manifest.

Not all nodes remain whole and complete throughout their existence. Some nodes spontaneously fragment after their emergence from the Dao. They do so for the same purpose that drives all nodes: to facilitate exploration and enhance their learning process.

Different nodes fragment into different numbers of fragments. There is a basic correlation between the size of the node and the number of its fragments. Larger nodes fragment into more nodes, smaller nodes into fewer. This is true as a general statement, but there are some exceptions. There is no need for us to describe the exceptions as they are not relevant to human experience.

Fragmentation that *is* relevant to human experience includes those nodes that co-associate with the human, as well as with the horse and the cetacean family, consisting of whales, dolphins and porpoises. These nodes do fragment. In the case of human beings and cetaceans, it is the individual fragments that occupy bodies, sequentially, one body at a time.

As regards numbers of fragments, nodes that co-associate with the human species fracture, on average, into one thousand individual fragments. This number is approximate. Some human-related nodes fracture into fewer fragments, some into more. Nodes that co-associate with horses and cetaceans fracture into fewer fragments than those that co-associate with the human.

Do all fragments of a node select to incarnate in the one species? Generally, yes. This is in part because they all receive the same advice from those who possess the same quality of Dao-nature. It is also because they wish to engage in their cycle of incarnations with those they know, these principally being other fragments of the same node, or fragments of other nodes closely associated with their own.

Nonetheless, some fragments do choose to co-associate with more than one species. And some select to co-associate with species on other planets completely, whether in this or in other galaxies. They may even explore opportunities offered by a species existing in a different universe. Selection is made entirely on the grounds that what is chosen offers useful and appropriate experiences.

Each node of Dao-consciousness possesses all the qualities of the Dao. These qualities include identity, intellect and purpose. Consequently, each individual fragment of a node also possesses identity, intellect and purpose. So you who are reading this transmission are a fragment of a node of Dao-consciousness. You have individual identity, intellect and purpose. You have self-creativity and choice. You have utilised these qualities to shape all your prior incarnations for the purpose of experiencing and learning. And you will continue to utilise them to evolve according to your self-creative intent.

Examining this process from a wider perspective, when a node of Dao-consciousness co-associates with a physical species it inevitably starts to learn certain things. It becomes aware of its place within the order of life. That includes developing a sense of its relationship to other levels within populations of nodes. And it acquires information, knowledge and understanding, as a result of which its opportunities for taking on responsibility are enhanced. It is through such experience that a node matures. And as it matures it becomes suited to explore more complex opportunities that are commensurate with its increasing maturity. This applies to all nodes, those that fragment and those that do not.

Fragmentation leads to another phenomenon that applies only to nodes that fragment. This is that at the end of their maturation cycles all of a node's fragments come back together to reunite and form what may be called the group soul. In the context of what we are now discussing, it can be said that the group soul is a reintegrated node of Dao-consciousness.

After all of a node's fragments have matured sufficiently, they are designated as having completed their cycles of reincarnation. They then reunite with every other fragment from the same node. In doing so, each brings back everything they have experienced and learned, every skill they have developed, the wisdom generated from every responsibility they have taken on and successfully negotiated. As a result, the node is incalculably enriched in comparison to its initial inexperienced state.

Underlying any and each exploration is the drive for enrichment: enrichment of the individual, enrichment of whatever environment a fragment occupies to which it can contribute, enrichment of the node when the stage of reunification is reached, and enrichment at other levels beyond that of the reunified node. The process of enrichment goes all the way back to the Dao, to which everything is eventually returned.

www.ingramcontent.com/pod-product-compliance
Lightning Source LLC
Chambersburg PA
CBHW020258030426
42336CB00010B/819